RELIGION AND SCIENCE:

CONFLICT AND SYNTHESIS

RELIGION AND SCIENCE

Conflict and Synthesis

Some Philosophical Reflections

by

IAN T. RAMSEY

*Nolloth Professor of the Philosophy of the Christian Religion
in the University of Oxford*

LONDON

S · P · C · K

1964

First published in 1964
by S.P.C.K.
Holy Trinity Church
Marylebone Road
London N.W.1

Made and printed in Great Britain by
William Clowes and Sons, Limited, London and Beccles

Contents

Preface

THIS book contains what are substantially the lectures I gave in 1960 as the fourth in the series of Annual Theological Lectures arranged by the Church of Ireland in the Queen's University, Belfast. I remember with particular gratitude all those who came through wintry nights of snow and ice to fill the Geology lecture-theatre with such a friendly and enthusiastic audience, and all those who offered me hospitality in the best Ulster traditions of abundant generosity. I am specially indebted to the Reverend Maurice Carey, Dean of Residences at Belfast, for all the care and thoughtfulness with which he planned my visit, and for what I was privileged to share of the worship, friendship, and discussion of the Chaplaincy Centre.

Informal discussion after the second lecture centred largely on the threat of cybernetics to a religious view of personality, and if I were rewriting the lectures this is a theme I would develop in much greater detail. Meanwhile, it is hardly possible to say much more in Chapter 2 without upsetting the general balance. But it happened subsequently that I was invited to join in a discussion on this same topic arranged in Oxford by the S.C.M. Study Secretary, and to comment on certain questions put in a very clear and challenging way by Mr Jonathan Dorling who was then studying psychology and philosophy at New College, Oxford. It seemed therefore that a record of this discussion might be usefully printed as a supplementary note to Chapter 2, especially since there is virtually nothing in this field which raises in a clear, simple, and challenging form issues which all Christians should be facing as best we can. Mr Dorling most kindly agreed that I might print his remarks even though they were written without any thought of publication.

It was also suggested that the sermon preached on Septuagesima in the Chaplaincy Church might be appropriately printed, and it follows the lectures as an epilogue although in time it preceded them. But I content myself with the thought that, after all, Ireland is a country where history rather than time is taken seriously.

Perhaps I ought to make it clear beyond misunderstanding that these three lectures were simply meant to focus on just one or two particular points about scientific method and one or two contemporary scientific issues where in my judgement the frontiers of science and religion meet. At the same time it was my hope that they would hint at the possibility of a synthesis. But the lectures were, of course, not meant to provide, and certainly did not provide, a complete philosophy of science.

Further, frontier work between various disciplines will always appear to some unsatisfactory, and I am as conscious as anyone of the many shortcomings which the following pages exhibit. At the same time it is essential for our academic, scientific, and indeed political, health that despite the risks of appearing superficial or stupid, more and more of us should venture into cross-fertilized discussions, and that dialogue should occur between different disciplines. It is in the hope that these lectures contain some suggestions which might help forward an ongoing discussion that they have been prepared for publication while retaining much of their original manner of presentation.

I.T.R.

Synopsis

ONE : *Need a Scientist be Religious ?*

1. Differing answers are associated with, e.g. Wilberforce, Huxley, and Ruskin; Newton and Laplace; Paley and Darwin.

2. Three possibilities for the relation of science and religion:
   a. That religion only provides labels for temporary scientific ignorance.
   b. That science and religion are different and distinct, being quite diverse activities.
   c. That science and religion, while each is characteristically distinctive, can nevertheless be harmonized in a single vision.

In this book we shall argue for the third possibility, and in this chapter examine in particular a feature of scientific method which argues for the kinship of religion and science.

3. Scientific method involves *inter alia* a search for invariants grounded in disclosures, e.g. "boiling point", "particle", "matter".

4. Three possible interpretations of these invariants:
   a. That they *describe* the "real" world. But then we have too much scientific furniture, some kinds of which are incompatible with others.
   b. That they are merely jingles, useful mnemonics to link different theories. But then it seems that the key concepts of science talk of nothing whatever.
   c. That they have somehow to be related to disclosures and to what disclosures disclose. But *what* do disclosures disclose?

5. Consider three examples of disclosures which disclose "persons", which are characterized by personal interchange. These may occur:

<ol type="a">
<li>a. Around a work of art.</li>
<li>b. When the active salesman is distinguished from his wax replica.</li>
<li>c. Around a succession of photographs.</li>
</ol>

6. To these three cases we can find parallels in science:
   <ol type="a">
   <li>a. A disclosure of beauty characterizing organic formulae and essentially involved in organic theory may suggest a personal interchange.</li>
   <li>b. Science uses personal concepts, e.g. rapport, harmony, opposition, in enunciating physical laws.</li>
   <li>c. The various models and pictures which in all their variegation comprise science may reveal something personal about the universe.</li>
   </ol>

Scientific method as a search for invariants is thus at *least compatible with* science regarded as a personal interchange between the scientist and the universe; and in this way the key concepts of science could find a basis in fact, a reference which other views either deny altogether or take too uncritically.

TWO: *What is Man?*

Our conclusion in Chapter 1—that science explicitly or implicitly makes use of a model of personal interchange—has a religious significance only if something about persons eludes the net of science. What, however, of the threat of contemporary science to human personality? This threat we discuss in three versions:

<ol type="a">
<li>a. There is the threat which arises out of large-scale developments in physics, viz. that man is an insignificant speck in the vast universe.</li>
<li>b. Another threat arises in a somewhat more complex manner out of developments in medicine. While religious men need not despair over the disappearance of the traditional soul-body dualism that made the development of scientific medicine possible, they face at the next move the threat that, even if physiological medicine is by itself insufficient, no more than psychological or psychosomatic medicine will be wanted. One way or another the</li>
</ol>

psychiatrist seems to challenge the priest as a "physician of the soul".

c. The third threat accompanies the development of cybernetics. The more complex a calculating machine, the closer may it approximate to the structure of the brain and the closer does its performance resemble human behaviour. Are men no more than complex machines?

Counter-arguments are then possible:

a. To see himself as a speck in a vast universe may just as well evoke man's wonder and worship, his sense of creaturely dependence, as his despair.

b. It is *not* necessary to suppose that psychiatric and religious ministrations are exclusive alternatives, e.g. with some illnesses *both* E.C.T. and religious ministrations may be needed.

c. While not denying the great advances in the study of the brain that developments in cybernetics have made possible, we may still claim that human behaviour is not a topic which cybernetics by itself can wholly exhaust. For (as is argued in more detail at the end of this chapter) each of us has a first-person subjectivity which is never—logically never—exhausted by any or all third-person accounts, of which cybernetics is one.

Such counter-arguments as these suggest then that a religious view of personality is still a live option.

Further, any denial of the religious significance of human personality brings with it several serious difficulties:

a. There seems to be no room left for the concept of responsibility, and, more generally, there seems to be a serious tension between the two foundations of modern society, law and science.

b. Individuality, eccentricity, and all distinctiveness of personality seem to be at a discount: a fact with serious implications for education.

Can we then argue for a religious view of personality? The argument starts from recognizing a fundamental logical difference between first and third person assertions which philosophers have for various reasons overlooked. A religious view of personality arises when we recognize that each of us is revealed to himself most distinctively in a "first-person" disclosure which, while it includes, is more than any and all "third-person" accounts—scientific accounts—of ourselves. Further, in such a personal disclosure there is not only a situation which *subjectively* assures us of our religious individuality, but *objectively* it is often a moral challenge, to which we answer and make an appropriate response as and when we behave responsibly. In this way we associate together, in a religious vision, both moral responsibility and scientific inquiry, and it is to such a religious vision we must turn if we wish to grasp fully and grapple with those crucial problems of our time which are both scientific and moral, e.g. atomic bombs and genetics; technology and automation; psychiatry and the law.

THREE: *Dare a Religious Man be a Scientist?*

In this chapter we consider a feature of scientific method which, it has been argued, is bound to make the scientist necessarily irreligious. This feature of scientific method, which some would say is dangerous for the religious man to practise, is experimental verification. There are three reasons why some religious people have been scandalized by this experimental method:

    a. It has been said to pander to man's selfish desire for human mastery.

    b. The scientist in his experimental method puts nature to the test, "extracting information by methods of the Inquisition".

    c. There is no theological parallel to the verifiable deduction which the experimental method involves.

It is this third point which deserves much the most serious consideration. We show with examples how what is *de rigueur* in theological reasoning thus becomes suspect in science; how what is suspect in science seems legitimate in theology.

In our further discussion of the experimental method in science:

    a. We readily recognize that the use of this method in science creates an important logical difference between the character of theological and scientific discourse.

b. Yet we also argue that these two diverse logical areas—
theology and science—*may* (and if we wish to have a single
language-map *must*) nevertheless be united.

Such a synthesis is to be made (we claim) by following logical
clues supplied by the behaviour of "I", when the basis in fact for
the synthesis will be those disclosures which for theology are a
sine qua non, and which even science presupposes (as we saw in
Chapter 1), though for its own day-to-day purposes it may
neglect them with impunity. Indeed, the important difference
which is spotlighted by the use of experimental verification in
science but not in theology, is a difference which, far from
registering an ultimate incompatibility (1) ensures that theology
has a logic peculiar enough to unite the fragmentary languages
of science without type-trespass, and (2) thus enables theology
to provide for a fragmented science the one cosmic map which
remains the scientific ideal. We thus approach a union of
theology and science which does justice to both, and which
compromises neither.

Religion thus gives to science the vision and single map for
which it searches; but science then pays the price of incorporating in the end categories, theological categories, which
elude empirical verification. Science gives to theology the
broad empirical relevance that it needs, providing theology
with a contemporary culture and moral problems on which it
can bring its insights to bear; but a theology with such broad
relevance cannot escape being tentative and reformable.

An illustration—the village fête—shows what these considerations come to in practice.

The chapter concludes with an appropriate tribute to George
Berkeley—sometime Dean of Derry, later Bishop of Cloyne—
who sponsored similar themes in an earlier day.

1

Need a Scientist be Religious?

IT is just over a century ago[1] since that notorious meeting of the British Association in the Science Museum at Oxford which saw the unedifying spectacle of Bishop Wilberforce taunting T. H. Huxley by asking, with what we are told was a smiling insolence, whether it was through his grandfather or his grandmother that he claimed his descent from a monkey. Huxley's devastating rejoinder is well known—he was not ashamed to have a monkey for his ancestor, but he would be ashamed to be connected with a man who used great gifts to obscure the truth.[2] The battle between science and religion was on.

Need a scientist be religious? The answer seemed to be: "No, and all the better if he were not." Yet this same Science Museum at Oxford, especially in its Gothic architecture, symbolized, for such a one as Ruskin,[3] a new synthesis, a culture at once ancient and modern, uniting the humanities and the sciences. Ruskin's vision may have been restricted. Technology, most disastrously, he placed outside the pale.[4] But, for Ruskin the scientist can be and must be a religious man, and will be when the vision of the artist unites them both. Need a scientist be religious? Ruskin would have said: "He is bound to be."

Let us now go back in time from the last century to a point some two hundred years earlier. What if we had put the question

---

[1] The meeting was in 1860.

[2] For further details see T. Seccombe and H. Spencer Scott, *In Praise of Oxford*, Vol. I, pp. 231f; *The Life and Letters of Thomas Huxley*, by Leonard Huxley; and I. T. Ramsey in *Leicester Cathedral Quarterly*, Vol. I, no. 1, pp. 12–17.

[3] See E. T. Cook, *The Life of Ruskin*, Vols. I and II, esp. Vol. I, pp. 450–3.

[4] Ibid., Vol. II, esp. p. 419.

to Isaac Newton? What if we look for an answer in his great *Principia Mathematica*, the very bible of classical physics? Need a scientist be religious? In the first edition the matter would seem to be left quite open. There is no mention of God anywhere. But in the second edition we find a very important General Scholium. "It is not to be conceived", said Newton in this Scholium, "that mere mechanical causes could give birth to so many regular motions", as he had described in the body of the work. "This most beautiful system of the sun, planets, and comets, could only proceed from the counsel and dominion of an intelligent and powerful Being."[1] In his *Opticks* he went even further, and taking the view that the interaction of man's body and mind took place at a part of the brain called the *sensorium*, Newton argued that Absolute Space might be thought to be the *sensorium* of God, the basis for God's activity in the world. So in Question 28 of his *Opticks*[2] we may read: "Does it not appear from Phænomena that there is a Being incorporeal, living, intelligent, omnipresent, who, in infinite Space, as it were in his Sensory, sees the things themselves intimately . . . and comprehends them wholly by their immediate presence to himself?" Here was physics completed in metaphysics. But, as Dr Mary Hesse aptly remarks in her *Science and the Human Imagination*,[3] while this might have been a very "sincere expression of faith on Newton's part", it had "no more to be said in its favour from a scientific point of view than had the atheism of the atomists". And this became abundantly clear, continues Dr Hesse, "when at the end of the eighteenth century Laplace succeeded in showing from the principle of gravitation itself, without making any additional assumptions, that the planetary system was, in fact, stable". One of the last scientific reasons for asserting the existence of God had disappeared. We all know how Laplace showed Napoleon the

---

[1] General Scholium to Book III, Proposition XLII. Sir Isaac Newton, *Mathematical Principles*, tr. A. Motte (1729), rev. and ed. F. Cajori (Berkeley, 1934), p. 544.

[2] Isaac Newton, *Opticks*, Book III, Qu. 28 (4th edn, corrected, London, 1730), p. 345.

[3] 1954, pp. 54f.

2

new edition of his *Mécanique Céleste*; how Napoleon asked him where God came in; and Laplace's answer, "Sir, I have no need of that hypothesis."[1] Need the scientist be religious? Laplace would have said, despite Newton, "No."

Journey back in time again, not this time in the direction of physics but in the direction of biology. Suppose we had put this question to William Paley, on whose *Evidences* so many Cambridge men were brought up.[2] Need the scientist be religious? "Yes, certainly," would have said Paley, "for how else would you account for the wonderful biological adaptations we find throughout nature?" As he says himself in his *Natural Theology*,[3] "in every nature and in every portion of nature which we can descry, we find attention bestowed upon even the minutest parts . . . the hinges in the wings of an *earwig* and the joints of its antennae, are as highly wrought, as if the Creator had nothing else to finish." Or let us think of the 446 known muscles cross-

[1] The story is recorded e.g. in W. W. Rouse Ball, *History of Mathematics*, p. 388.

[2] And many others, too. For example, an introduction to a popular edition of Paley's *Evidences* (Ward, Lock & Co., paper back, 1s., about 1881) designed for "Ministers and Teachers" and "Christian Heads of Households", edited by a certain F. A. Maeleson, comments: "The manly force, the clear incisive statement of truth by Dr Paley, supply at least one unanswerable demonstration against these modern apostles of doubt and disbelief." It is true that all this relates to Paley's *Evidences* and not his *Natural Theology*, but Paley was a great popularizer of a world-view which comprised both natural and revealed theology, both the argument from design and the Bible. Incidentally, Paley's *Evidences* only ceased to be a prescribed book in "Little-go" (the Previous Examination of Cambridge University) in 1920, the last paper being set on 9 December in that year.

[3] *Natural Theology*, ch. 27. Conclusion—in *Works*, ed. A. Chalmer (1821), Vol. IV, p. 423. See also, for example, ibid., ch. 9, p. 114: "Keill has reckoned up, in the human body, 446 muscles, dissectable and describable; and hath assigned a use to every one of the number. This cannot be all imagination." Again, cf. ch. 11, p. 163, where he says of *poultry*: "and in this position it sleeps in safety; for the claws do their office in keeping hold of the support, not by any exertion of voluntary power, which sleep might suspend, but by the traction of the tendons in consequence of the attitude which the legs and thighs take by the bird sitting down, and to which the mere weight of the body gives the force that is necessary."

ing, perforating, and enveloping one another—what a wonderful, intricate, and ingenious pattern; or, when fowls go to roost, look at the arrangements which enables them to close their claws as they bend their legs. Is not God's meditation and counsel plain, obvious, and striking? Or, to go from the farmyard to the city hall, consider the city aldermen at some great dinner, with both quantity and variety of food in abundance. Recall that it is the epiglottis which alone, and in the most marvellous way, prevents them from choking on every mouthful. Need the scientist be religious? No question of it. So much in the universe registers and is evidence for the purposive hand of God.

Then came Charles Darwin with an alternative explanation. Aldermen did not choke at their city dinner because every prehistoric alderman with a different epiglottis had choked already. It was merely a special case of the survival of the fittest. The fowls who roosted imperfectly had been obliterated in the struggle for existence. Men with less or more than 446 muscles had perished in the rush. Earwigs with imperfect hinges had been bred out. Nature had its own technique of natural selection. There was no need to talk of God's purposes or to introduce the concept of God at all. As with Laplace, so with Darwin. Not only physics but now biology as well could dispense with God. God seemed to have been carried away on the flood-tide of scientific progress.

Now there are three possible reflections on such scientific developments as I have just outlined.

a. First, religion, it might be said, is a phenomenon which is bound to disappear in a scientific age; that the themes of religion are progressively excluded as science advances. A rainbow appears in the sky and Noah, as in Genesis 9.13, sees it as God's bow. But along comes the physicist. He sees it as an occasion for telling a different story, a story about the composite character of white light, refraction and reflection in a spherical shell, and so on. Or thunder—at one time maybe, God's voice in the heavens,[1] but now merely the inrush of air following on that electrical discharge known as lightning. Religious themes,

[1] See John 12.28,29.

4

on this first view, might possibly provide convenient currency for unchartered scientific areas. Religion might provide convenient labels for temporary scientific ignorance. But sooner or later these religious labels would become, on this view, superfluous. God is bound to abdicate, indeed we might say to disappear altogether, in the face of scientific progress. Developments in nuclear research at one end, the investigation of interplanetary space at the other, and all those exciting borderline subjects like biochemistry and biophysics—all these mean the complete erosion of religion. On this view the total disappearance of religion is merely a matter of time as (to change the metaphor) the scientific tentacles spread. That is one possible conclusion as we reflect on the development of the relations between science and religion over the last century.

b. There is then a second and different view. We are wrong, it might be said, in ever trying to link science and religion, for "religion" describes an altogether different and distinctive activity from science. The truth is—and many colleagues might rejoice to know it—that scientists on principle should have no dealings with the theologians. Here are two quite separate human activities, and whether anybody displays both depends merely on a man's particular whims and fancies. Some scientists, in their spare time, may like to be religious; others might not. Some may sit with their feet up, while others go for a walk. Some may vote for "draught"; others would vote for "bottled", Well, what of it? Need the scientist be religious? Not at all—he must merely please himself.

c. Now I will return to those two quite different reactions in Chapter 3. Meanwhile I would like to set before you another possibility. What I want to suggest in these lectures is a third view—a view of science and religion which recognizes their distinctive features, so avoiding that kind of homogeneity that is implied in alternative *a*, but also recognizes the need and possibility to comprise them in one vision, so avoiding the kind of dichotomy behind alternative *b*. On this view, while science and religion have each their characteristically different features, they can nevertheless, as I shall argue, be harmonized in an outlook on life which genuinely combines both. The synthetic

5

vision of a Ruskin, nay more, a vision more comprehensive than Ruskin's, because it will, I hope, include technology, may yet prove to be possible.

In this first chapter I shall try to draw out some of the wider implications of science which may have a religious significance. Whether they have or not is a question which leads us into the controversial issues of Chapter 2; but the greatest challenge which must be faced by anyone who seeks a kinship between science and religion is reserved for Chapter 3. Does not the experimental verification of deductions from hypotheses constitute a distinctive feature of scientific method, which makes the approaches of science and religion utterly diverse and quite incompatible? This is the crucial question to be faced at the end by those who, like myself, plead for a single vision, for a synthetic relating of religion and science.

I am not so silly as to suppose that such a family of methods, such a complex methodology as we call scientific, can be reduced to a few characteristic features, but for the purpose of illustrating and arguing my case I have, in fact, selected from scientific method two features. One of these, which I reserve for Chapter 3, ostensibly argues, as I have hinted, for the diversity of science and religion. But the feature of scientific method I propose to discuss in this chapter, argues rather, on the other side, for the kinship of religion and science. What will concern us here is the part played in science by intuition, or what we may call "disclosures".

Let us first notice that scientific method is, *inter alia*, a search for invariants, a search for some order and some constant pattern in the diverse events of the spatio-temporal world around us. Science aims at linking apparently diverse phenomena together and, in providing such links, mathematics is of the first importance. We may take three illustrations.

a. First suppose we do a simple third-form experiment with water. We heat several beakers until the water in each boils; until the temperature, as measured on some thermometer, becomes steady, and we then note the temperatures as registered by the several thermometers in the several beakers and set them down, as it were, on a graph:

6

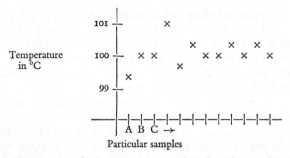

Particular samples

I am exaggerating the variation somewhat, but the result might be something like that. Now suppose we had not done this experiment before, and we did not know what the answer was or even how to reach it. It might then help if we first recalled something vastly different from the lab.—the lounge on a wet afternoon when we had the children to entertain. We might recall a child's drawing-book with a series of dots on one page like this:

To make the game last longer than usual, I suggest that, instead of joining the dots by lines, we might put dots between the first dots; dots between all the dots now on the paper, and so on—repeating the process until . . . What? Until, suddenly, there occurs a disclosure, and we see not just dots but a picture, (say) Telford's suspension bridge over the Menai Straits.

Now let us have an exercise not quite so childish. Let us start with the following group (1) of dots:

(1) .   .   .   .

(2) . .   .   .   .

     a   b   c

7

Play the game as before. What happens after adding 3 dots a, b, and c as in (2)? Perhaps the answer will be: nothing whatever. So insert more dots between the 7 dots. What happens? Again, nothing particular may happen. Let us insert, and insert, and insert again: until what? The hope is that at some point or other the light will dawn, the penny drop, and we will say, "By jove, a straight line." Now, we cannot strictly speaking draw a straight line. We may draw a chalk mark or a pencil mark or an ink mark, but not a straight line. By the phrase "a straight line" we label what is revealed in the disclosure which occurs around the dots, dots, and more dots, something which, when the disclosure occurs, absorbs all the dots to date and any number of dots—no matter how great. When a disclosure occurs around the dots, no matter how many or how few we have drawn, we say that we "see" "a straight line".[1]

Now let us go back to the water-boiling experiment. Remember the dots in that case. Perhaps nothing strikes us. If not, recall the children's game and produce more dots. In short, repeat the experiment—boil water, water, and yet more water until around the dots we have an intuition, and a straight line is disclosed. We link the various dots together in a pattern, and we associate this pattern with the one which discloses "a straight line". We now register the line as symbolizing 100° Centigrade. Incidentally, we are extremely lucky in our laboratory equipment if *all* the thermometers have read exactly 100° Centigrade; and even if they do, a few lenses, through which to peer at the mercury column, will ensure that we have eventually an irregular set of dots. But in any case it will still be by a process of intuition that we see a series of dots—regular or irregular—making up "a straight line", and speak of 100° Centigrade as the boiling-point of water. Here then is a scientific invariant rooted in a disclosure. Something dawns on us—100°C—as the straight line dawned on us, and this we take to be our invariant in relation to the terms—boiling-temperatures of water—which evoked the disclosure.

b. A second example: think of the scientific concept of a

[1] The phrase may of course also label what is revealed in the disclosure which occurs around a group of pencil and chalk or ink lines.

point particle, a concept that blights so many lives struggling for senior or junior certificates. Now, what are point particles? This phrase, too—"point particle"—is, I suggest, rooted in a disclosure. Set down a series of declining shapes such as this:

and what happens? It may be that nothing whatever happens, as we saw could well be the case with the child's drawing-book. But it is always possible, if we continue far enough, that at some stage or other there will be a disclosure, that "the penny will drop". What we are aware of when this disclosure occurs— that which, as A. N. Whitehead pointed out,[1] will include all those spatial areas and, I would add, many more besides—what strikes us objectively at the moment of disclosure, spatial areas and more, is what is meant by the phrase "a point particle". The word "particle" labels what is revealed in the disclosure evoked by that particular group of shapes; we give the name "particle" to what strikes us when we play successfully that kind of game.[2]

c. So to a third example by way of illustrating how scientific invariants are grounded in disclosures. Suppose for the sake of argument that there are no particular difficulties in measuring the force acting on a body and its resultant acceleration. We might then have another series of dots,[3] from which could arise another straight line. If it did, we would then claim to "see" that the force acting on a particular body, divided by the acceleration produced, is a constant, just as we "saw" that the temperature of water boiling under normal conditions was constant: $100°C$.

[1] *The Concept of Nature* (1919), ch. 4; *Process and Reality* (1928), Part 4 ch. 2, esp. s. III.

[2] However strange and complex this may seem as an account of a particle, I may add that it totally accords with Whitehead's view.

[3] As we would have if we did e.g. a Fletcher's Trolley experiment.

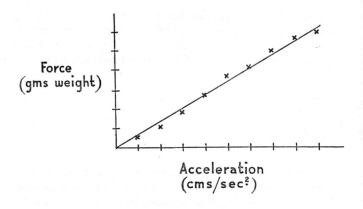

Force
(gms weight)

Acceleration
(cms/sec²)

We would then have discovered—I need not go into the details—another invariant. Here, grounded in another disclosure, would be another scientific category. This time what is revealed is "mass"—a concept attached to a certain insight, a certain disclosure, one which occurs in this way around the behaviour of a particular object in certain circumstances.

Now at this stage further discussion of invariants such as boiling-point, particle, or mass might proceed along three possible paths, the first two of which, deliberately or not, ignore the significance of what I have called disclosures.

It might be said that some, or all, of these invariants merely *describe*, and straightforwardly describe, something or other. It sounds eminently sensible on a bitterly cold night to say that "temperature" describes a certain feature of the air or pavement outside. Consequently people begin to say, "If temperature describes a feature of something (as it surely does) isn't the same true for 'particle' or 'mass' or 'absolute space' or 'entropy'?" If one such word describes something, surely the others do? And then we get darkened counsel. Mass (it is suggested) is some sort of mysterious and rather elusive property belonging to bodies, somehow related to, but not identical with, their weight. As for a particle, a particle is thought of as a delightfully invisible teeny-weeny lump of mysterious stuff which does all sorts of exciting things. But of course the trouble on this view, this descriptive view, is that as science develops and invariants change, the world becomes cluttered up with scientific furniture of the most extraordinary sort. The old hard particles have a very uneasy relationship and existence with and among electrons, protons, mesons, and the rest. And what about those wave mechanics, as well as particle mechanics? When these make their necessary appearance—oh dear, what can the matter be? The world must be waves, and the world must be particles and surely it cannot be both. Nothing can be both clear, shivering jelly, and lumpy sago pudding at the same time. Hence, even though this first view has had great popularity, and has been held by most eminent scientists, it is a great temptation, when all these difficulties arise, for other scientists to say, by reaction, "Away with the pictures altogether. A plague on supposing scientific language to be descriptive." "Absolute space", "absolute time", such phrases no more label things than did the word "Ether", that darling of nineteenth-century physicists. How ridiculous to ask what entropy is!—as though $\int dH/\theta$ could label anything at all. And so by reaction we pass to the second possibility.

We are now at the opposite extreme—far from being labels, invariant words talk about nothing whatever. Scientific invariants are now merely jingles or typographical devices which in themselves refer to nothing whatever. They are all given operationally, and some would say: "Be content to work with, and to look for nothing beyond, the whole variety of techniques that these invariants specify." If I understand them aright, that is the view of the Copenhagen School. Here are many complementary schemes, let us merely opt for what suits us, for whatever is at the moment best suited to some particular purpose or experiment. Others, like Bohm,[1] go beyond the Copenhagen School, at least in so far as they essay some sort of unity by looking for what they call "hidden parameters" which might somehow or other link the various mnemonics, jingles, or typographical devices. But such complications do not at

[1] See e.g. D. Bohm, *Causality and Chance in Modern Physics* (1957).

present matter for us, because as Heisenberg remarks in a *Festschrift* for Niels Bohr, when he considers various alternatives to "the Copenhagen interpretation", "it is (in any event) impossible" to return "to the idea of an objective real world, whose smallest parts exist objectively in the same way as stones and trees".[1] But what then is science about? The labelling view makes science talk about too much; on such a view there is too much scientific furniture in the world. Yet, on this alternative view, it almost looks as though we have no scientific furniture at all. Here is a real problem. From supposing that scientific invariants label, describe, or picture the real world, and then finding that no consistent picture could be built up—we are given too much and quite incompatible furniture—it becomes a temptation to say that the invariants are just jingles, having no significance whatever beyond the spatio-temporal phenomena they usefully organize and bring together. But *are* scientific invariants devoid of any significance? Are the invariants, which are the very basis of scientific method, talking about nothing at all besides the observations they conveniently organize and link together? Must we not try to salvage *something* from the older labelling view? Can we not say that these invariants of science, in some way or another, are clues to the real world? Can we not say that in some way or another they talk distinctively about something, though they do *not* talk about little teeny-weeny particles, or big whopping absolute spaces?

To answer these questions, let us recall what both of these views left out of account. They omitted, you remember, the disclosure, the intuition. Deliberately or not, they omitted from consideration what I claimed to be an essential part of the contextual setting of scientific invariants. Therefore, if we are looking for some kind of distinctive reference for these invariants, if we are interested to know more fully what they are about, and what science talks about when it uses them, if we

[1] W. Pauli *et al.*, eds., *Niels Bohr and the Development of Physics. Essays dedicated to Niels Bohr on the occasion of his seventieth birthday* (1955), essay by W. Heisenberg, "The Development of the Interpretation of the Quantum Theory", p. 17.

are anxious to make the central concepts of science more than mere typographical devices; if we do not want the astonishing pseudo-metaphysical furniture with which the labelling view fills the world, yet at the same time wish to salvage something for science without having these metaphysical monstrosities, is it not reasonable to look around to see what disclosure language talks about elsewhere? In order to salvage something for science, why not ask: where else do we find disclosures? Where else do we find disclosures reminiscent of those which, if I am right, are to be associated with scientific invariants? If we ask ourselves these questions, if we ask where we may find disclosures which might give us a line on what science talks about, which will help us to mediate between the two opposite and unsatisfactory views we have examined so far; if we ask ourselves where do we find disclosures which in some way might yield clues for talking about a scientific disclosure, my answer will be: *in characteristically personal situations*. But that is to anticipate.

What I wish to do now is to take just three examples of other disclosures, personal disclosures, which on the face of it might look far removed from science; three disclosures which might seem miles away from scientific method. Whether they are, we will see presently.

a. First, suppose we look at a picture. It may well seem to us, particularly if it is a recent picture, no more than a series of daubs: one daub after another. No disclosure; no penny-dropping; no insight. But it may happen that on some occasion —perhaps because for a moment we associate that picture with some particular object or circumstance which both the artist and ourselves know—a disclosure occurs. We may then find in that picture, in that series of daubs, some personal rapport with the artist. Some object or situation has come alongside it, and out of a series of daubs with such images as a catalyst, a disclosure occurs, the picture becomes evocative of a personal interchange. We might say, generalizing, that surrealist art becomes significant as and when we somehow associate the daubs with certain objects, and thus build up a pattern of such a kind that it generates a disclosure, a disclosure which reveals, as would be said, the artist's mind, or I prefer to say, the artist's personality. So it is that complex relations between paint daubs, at least in certain contexts, that "colour" and "form" tell us of what philosophers of aesthetics call *empathy*, a fellow-feeling between the artist and ourselves. When impersonal daubs become the beautiful, they have evoked a personal rapport.

b. For our second example of a personal disclosure, let us imagine a visit to some engineering exhibition where, pulled by the children rather than by our pockets, we gravitate to the Rolls-Royce stand. We see two men sitting resplendent at a table in a truly magnificent setting. "Ah", we whisper to the boys, "just notice: they're models." We have looked at them a good deal beforehand and have seen them as waxy, immobile, highly coloured. "You are sure they are models?" the boys ask. "Well", we say, "notice: whatever anyone does, whoever approaches them, there's no genuine rapport, no sign either of harmony or opposition. Look here!", and, very bold, we go to one, push him, and we would knock him over did we not drag him back by a lapel to his seat. Proof perfect. But what if, on approaching the other to repeat the experiment, this second one suddenly springs to life and rises to shake us by the hand?—a disclosure indeed! Further, suppose that after the handshake, as we go to inspect the engine on display at the stand, he moves with us. Here is undoubted rapport. When we utter some particular words, he hands us pamphlets—here is positive harmony; but when we have failed to press the clutch-pedal down, he prevents us from trying the gears—here is opposition. In these three ways the claim of our disclosure to reveal a person, to reveal personal interchange, is justified. With the man we nearly knocked over, who was indeed wax and powder, there was no disclosure, nothing came alive. There was neither rapport, nor positive harmony, nor opposition.

c. For the third example of a personal disclosure, suppose we are in a hotel lounge on a wet afternoon and an acquaintance takes from her handbag various photographs: two, three, four, five, six. . . . It *may* be that at some particular point in the sequence, all at once, as with the dots in the drawing-book, a disclosure occurs—the person makes himself known to us, he "stands out" from the photographs, as we would say. Presented with various pictures of Roger eating, Roger dancing, Roger bathing, Roger in shorts, Roger in flannels, and so on, we may in this way come to know Roger, whereas with one photograph and "There's my boy-friend", Roger may be no more than a two-dimensional façade. With a number of Roger-appearances put together, the penny may drop, we may come to know the "real Roger". There will then be a disclosure of the personality of which the photographs are façades. Alternatively, after being given one or two pictures, our acquaintance may look up and suddenly remark, "And here's Roger!" At that point, as we too look up, a disclosure may occur, and if it does, it is once again something which incorporates all and every two-dimensional façade we have seen or could ever see: once again we know the "real Roger", the "living Roger". Other-wise, if there happens to be no disclosure, on looking up we merely see what the photographs picture, and what a sufficient number of façades, photographic or otherwise, could adequately represent.

Here then are disclosures, in what appears *prima facie* to be a vastly different context from that of science, and it might be said that it will be a *non sequitur* to argue that the disclosure of scientific invariants bespeaks likewise a personal interchange. It might be said that it is as much a *non sequitur* as it would be a *non sequitur* to argue that everybody in a white coat in hospital is a doctor, because some are. But supposing somebody now shows us that, in one or two particular cases something in a white coat that we should never have expected to be a doctor, is nevertheless a doctor in fact. Then the generalization would at least be more plausible. Well, that is the suggestion which I am making here. What if these characteristically personal situations have in fact, however unexpectedly, scientific echoes? What if that most unlikely fellow in the white coat proves indeed to be a doctor of medicine? What if these personal situations, ostensibly so different from the scientific cases, have nevertheless scientific echoes?

Next, then, let us see how, in each of the cases we have mentioned so far, scientific echoes are to be found. I propose to take three examples, corresponding to each of the cases I mentioned of distinctively personal situations.

a. First, we had the artistic disclosure of beauty, the aesthetic appreciation of colour and form. Let us see a scientific echo in a few simple examples from organic chemistry. The organic chemist, as we would expect, has his invariants and some of these invariants he shares quite gladly with his inorganic colleagues. These are the symbols for atoms; C for carbon, H for hydrogen, O for oxygen, and the rest. Thus for the organic chemist, as well as for the inorganic chemist, C represents an invariant, something which is common between such ostensibly different objects as soot, graphite, coal, and Lady Docker's diamonds. But the organic chemist is not even satisfied with that disclosure of far-reaching invariancy. The organic chemist would not think he had made much progress if he had nothing beyond that kind of invariant, since thousands, if not millions, of the situations with which he deals all need these symbols, C, H, O, and not many others. A formula of the form $C_xH_yO_z$ is not going to be very much use when the range of x, y, and z is so vast and variable, and especially when (as we shall see) *different* compounds may have the *same* values for x and y and z. The organic chemist, therefore, needs desperately other invariants, and it is in the choice of these other invariants that considerations of beauty and form and shape arise.

Consider e.g. the formula $C_2H_4O_2$. No organic chemist is going to be content with a formula such as that. He will not be content even with a formula such as CH_3COOH which spreads itself out a little more and where considerations of spatial position and form have already played their part in the symbolism. He will be content only with a formula such as, in this case, is written:

$$
\begin{array}{c}
\text{H} \\
| \\
\text{H--C--C--O--H} \\
| \quad \| \\
\text{H} \quad \text{O}
\end{array}
$$

Here is a formula which is quite unashamedly spatial. Nor is he

16

just being obtuse when he wants a formula written like that. For this insight into form and pattern is going to help him to see kinship between his

$$\begin{array}{c} \quad\quad\; H \\ \quad\quad\; | \\ H-C-C-O-H \\ \quad\; | \quad\; || \\ \quad\; H \quad O \end{array}$$

—acetic acid—and what can be symbolized as this:

$$\begin{array}{c} H-C-O-H \\ \quad || \\ \quad O \end{array}$$

—formic acid—and between both these and what can be symbolized as this:

$$\begin{array}{c} \quad\; H \;\; H \\ \quad\; | \quad\; | \\ H-C-C-C-O-H \\ \quad\; | \quad\; | \quad\; || \\ \quad\; H \;\; H \;\; O \end{array}$$

—propionic acid—and so on. The pattern will in fact reliably symbolize the family of the "fatty acids" $(C_nH_{2n+1}COOH)$. In other words, for the organic chemist, the discernment of beauty and form is integrally implied in scientific method itself. It is no kind of extraneous consideration. The very form represents a scientific invariant. The inorganic invariants such as C, H, and O are not enough for the organic chemist. Form and structure are absolutely basic and essential to his theory. A disclosure of beauty is embedded in his utterances. The universe speaks to him through e.g. the fatty acids, as the artist discloses himself to us in an artistic creation.

As a second and more particular example of the same point consider toluene C_7H_8, represented spatially as a derivative of benzene C_6H_6 itself, which written spatially around a hexagon is:

$$\begin{array}{c} \quad\; CH \\ HC \diagup\;\;\diagdown CH \\ \;\; | \quad\quad\; | \\ HC \diagdown\;\;\diagup CH \\ \quad\; CH \end{array}$$

In the case of toluene one "CH" group is replaced by "C_2H_3" so that we write it:

$$\begin{array}{c} \text{C--CH}_3 \\ \text{HC} \underset{\text{HC}}{\bigcirc} \text{CH} \\ \text{CH} \end{array} \quad or \quad \begin{array}{c} \text{CH}_3 \\ \bigcirc \end{array}$$

as it is customarily written. Suppose now we carry out the process known as sulphonation. The result is not just one product, but two very similar products. "How on earth", says the organic chemist, "can we represent the invariant there, when we get two different compounds from the same process?" And the answer is: appeal a second time to spatial consideration.

Here is toluene:

$$\begin{array}{c} \text{CH}_3 \\ \bigcirc \end{array}$$

and the suggestion is that sulphonation results in the replacement of a second hydrogen atom by the "SO_3H" group. We might of course write the result $C_7H_8SO_3$. But how then do we distinguish the *two* products of the reaction? Once again we appeal *as part of scientific theory* to spatial considerations, and the two cases are represented by

$$\begin{array}{c} \text{CH}_3 \\ \bigcirc\!\!^{\text{SO}_3\text{H}} \end{array} \quad and \quad \begin{array}{c} \text{CH}_3 \\ \bigcirc \\ \text{SO}_3\text{H} \end{array}$$

No jiggery-pokery in the world will make those two symbols identical in the way that (say)

$$\begin{array}{c} \text{CH}_3 \\ \text{H}_2\text{N}\,\bigcirc \end{array} \quad and \quad \begin{array}{c} \text{CH}_3 \\ \bigcirc\,\text{NH}_2 \end{array}$$

are, despite appearances, spatially identical. Yet the earlier pair differ only in their form, in their artistic patterning. The difference is something which is disclosed only to an eye which is an eye for beauty. If a person cannot distinguish one point of a hexagon from another, he will not appreciate this scientific argumentation at all. But if he does, the distinction enables him both to distinguish and to relate ortho-toluene sulphuric acid and para-toluene sulphonic acid, and in fact sulphonation can now be said to produce 40% of the ortho-acid, and 60% of the para-acid. Here are spatial considerations functioning as an essential part of the theory of isomers, and we may note that there could in theory be a meta-toluene sulphonic acid:

$$CH$$

$$\langle \rangle SO_3H$$

We may also note that spatial considerations play an even more far-reaching part in what is known as stereo-isomerism. Here e.g. with a substance such as β-methylbutan-α-ol:

$$C_2H_5 \qquad\qquad H$$

$$C$$

$$CH_3 \qquad\qquad CH_2OH$$

where we have a carbon atom whose four valencies are satisfied by four different atoms or groups, two versions of the compound are spatially distinguished as (i) a tetrahedron where the groups are respectively placed at its four corners and (ii) its mirror image. This is said to offer a "perfectly sound and rational explanation"[1] of why one isomer rotates the plane of polarization to the left, another rotates it to the right, and the third—an equal mixture of both—is optically inactive.

In such ways, then, as organic chemistry theorizes more and more, more and more does it make use of spatial considerations as an integral part of its method, and *not* merely as a psychological aid to teaching, a sort of primitive exercise in visual aid. The spatial formulae of organic chemistry *are* that; but that is not their only, and certainly not their most important, defence.

[1] As in L. A. Coles, *An Introduction to Modern Organic Chemistry* (1955), p. 149.

Returning now to our main theme, may not these spatial formulae, artistic creations necessitated by scientific method itself, by their very form evoke a personal disclosure? May not organic formulae, by their very artistic form, become symbols of a personal interchange with the universe? Creations of the organic chemist they may be: but they arise from his interchange with the universe, and can give that interchange a personal character.

Lastly, consider mutton fat. How unpromising, you might think, as a symbol of personal interchange. But suppose that an invariant in mutton fat can be represented by what results, besides water, from linking three molecules of stearic acid with one of glycerol, the whole reaction being spatially represented as follows:

$$
\begin{array}{l}
\quad\quad\quad\quad\ \overset{\displaystyle O}{\overset{\|}{}} \quad\quad\quad\quad\quad \overset{\displaystyle H}{\overset{|}{}} \\
C_{17}H_{35}-C-O\ |\ H \quad HO\ |-C-H \\[2ex]
\quad\quad\quad\quad\ \overset{\displaystyle O}{\overset{\|}{}} \\
C_{17}H_{35}-C-O\ |\ H \quad HO\ |-C-H \\[2ex]
\quad\quad\quad\quad\ \overset{\displaystyle O}{\overset{\|}{}} \\
C_{17}H_{35}-C-O\ |\ H \quad HO\ |-C-H \\
\quad\quad\quad\quad\quad\quad\quad\quad\quad\quad\quad\quad\quad \overset{|}{H}
\end{array}
$$

stearic acid   glycerol

whereupon we have the following wonderful space formula:

$$
\begin{array}{l}
\quad\quad\quad\quad\ \overset{\displaystyle O}{\overset{\|}{}} \quad \overset{\displaystyle H}{\overset{|}{}} \\
C_{17}H_{35}-C-O-C-H \\[2ex]
\quad\quad\quad\quad\ \overset{\displaystyle O}{\overset{\|}{}} \\
C_{17}H_{35}-C-O-C-H \\[2ex]
\quad\quad\quad\quad\ \overset{\displaystyle O}{\overset{\|}{}} \\
C_{17}H_{35}-C-O-C-H \\
\quad\quad\quad\quad\quad\quad\quad\ \overset{|}{H}
\end{array}
$$

The glyceride Tristearin

When this is seen as an invariant in mutton fat, mutton fat not only bespeaks a beauty of form, but becomes thereby a possible purveyor of an artistic disclosure; besides which, that very formulation, as any biochemist will agree, helps to forward in particular the theory of digestion. Once again, the disclosure of personal rapport by artistic beauty, which seemed miles away from the techniques of science, can be integrally associated with organic theory.

b. What then of the second kind of personal disclosure—that which arose at the Rolls-Royce stand—that which was associated with rapport, harmony, opposition. Look for an echo this time in physics. Take first, Newton's Third Law: that action and reaction are opposite and equal. What could be better currency for mutual harmony and rapport? May not Newton's Third Law, then, be a clue to, hint at, be grounded in, a personal disclosure?

Secondly, what of the principle of resonance, which tells us how sympathetic rhythms generate enormous vibrations, so that soldiers break step on the bridge, while scientific children give their swings regular impulses at appropriate points. Here is the language of harmony indeed. May it not be, then, that the principle of resonance is scientific language for a harmony which hints at a personal disclosure? To put it otherwise, when the scientific child on his swing deliberately gives it an impulse at just the right time, so that the swing goes wider and wider and higher and higher, not only may he read into his success the principle of resonance, he may also, on that swing, find God in the universe.

Or, thirdly, opposition. Perhaps we may mention two echoes, one in physics, the other in physical chemistry. What about Lenz's Law in physics? This law generalizes about circumstances which may be expressed crudely as follows. If we "induce" a current in a coil by bringing up a magnet, the current flows in a direction such that the magnetic field associated with it resists the advance of the magnet any further. More precisely the law could be formulated: An induced current always flows in such a direction as to oppose the action inducing it. Here is co-ordinated opposition, negative rapport between the universe and the physicist. Again, what of Le Chatelier's Principle—that any change in the conditions of a system in equilibrium causes the equilibrium to be displaced in such a direction as to oppose the effects of the change? Colourful physics and chemistry masters call these laws "the laws of pure cussedness". Certainly they bespeak co-ordinated opposition. But may not Lenz's Law and Le Chatelier's Principle on that very account be scientific hints at, and clues to, what can be more broadly regarded as personal disclosures?

c. Lastly, let us recall the photograph example. To find an echo in science, let us begin by reminding ourselves of the various models, the various languages, and perhaps even the associated pictures of which scientific method has made and still makes use. The Atomic Theory gave us a universe of atoms, what has been called a billiard-ball universe, and the Kinetic Theory, which regards gases as made up of molecules behaving largely in accordance with the equations of classical mechanics, belongs to the same family. Here are models of far-reaching scientific significance. Or there is the theory of heat conduction and, even more obviously, the theory of electrical transmission developed on the model not of billiard-ball atoms but of fluid flow whereby we speak of heat or a current "flowing". Finally, to take one example in a little more detail, when sodium burns in chlorine to form crystalline sodium chloride, one way of symbolizing it is:

$$2Na + Cl_2 = 2NaCl$$

i.e. we may speak of two atoms of sodium and one of chlorine joining to give two molecules of sodium chloride. This would once have been a good and sufficient story about the reaction. A little later, however, chemistry books spoke of the sodium atom transferring an electron to the chlorine atom. This was a rather picturesque way of mixing pictures, with atomic language and electron language brought together into the same sentence. But as considerations of stringency and rigour prevailed, the symbolic representation became:

$$Na^{\circ} + \underset{x x}{\overset{x x}{x\ \overset{}{Cl}}}\ \overset{x}{\underset{x}{\ }} \rightarrow Na^{\circ}_{x}\ \underset{x x}{\overset{x x}{Cl}}\ \overset{x}{\underset{x}{\ }}$$

when the story is in terms of electrons alone, symbolized as $\circ$ and $\times$. Here is some indication of the vast variety of scientific pictures and models.

Now it is quite true that people like Bohm, as I have already mentioned, have been dissatisfied with all this diversification, and in particular have endeavoured to unite wave mechanics and particle mechanics, by hidden parameters. People like Bohm might, in principle, still hope in their heart of hearts for one homogeneous treatment of science, for one story which could be labelled as true science. But I am bound to say that when Bohm endeavours to do that, as hidden parameters endeavour to do in a particular case, my guess is that what he will finish with is no homogeneous reconciliation, but rather a third more comprehensive model, a third story to set along-side wave and particle mechanics, a story which by no means disposes of or homogeneously links the other two. So we have: many models, many pictures, many languages, many mathematical techniques. Well, just as the photographs, may they not "click" in respect to their subject? May they not disclose that which is their common topic, what they might indeed have called the "real world"? If so, there is some reason to talk of this "real world" which they disclose as something which declares itself in what is closely similar to a personal encounter.

Now to where have these various reflections led? They have led up to this point, that scientific method and procedure, in so far as it is concerned with invariants, is at least consistent with a personal view of the universe—and I deliberately put it no stronger than that.[1] Not that much more might not be said. To take only one further point. Such a view as is suggested by these reflections would certainly give, for instance, a much-

[1] In this connection the reader may wish to consult M. Polanyi, *Personal Knowledge* (1958), where a stronger form of this conclusion, viz. that scientific knowledge demands "personal participation", is reached after a detailed and scholarly discussion of the character of scientific knowledge.

needed basis for information theory in physics. On such a theory the universe gives the physicist answers only in terms of the language which he himself feeds into it. But what is the fundamental implication of that, if not that science is, at its best, a dialogue with the universe, a personal interchange with what is revealed to us in a disclosure?

What, then, is my conclusion? Need the scientist be religious? If the scientist needs to be religious, it will be, on what I have said in this chapter, because personal disclosures justify religious categories. But do they? Even if, as I have tried to argue, scientific method and procedures suggest and can be harmonized with a personal model, the scientist need not be religious unless "person" is a religious category. Is it? What is man? That is the question I consider in my next chapter. Meanwhile, let me summarize the argument to this point.

I started by recalling the Wilberforce–Huxley controversy, and we looked at the classical answers of scientists and others to the question "Need the scientist be religious?" Newton and Paley and Ruskin were on the one side, Laplace and Darwin were on the other. We then noted three possible views of the relation between science and religion. The first would hold that the exclusion of religion by the progress of science is inevitable, and that religious truth is only tolerable in times of scientific ignorance. On the second view there would be a basic dichotomy between science and religion. We shall give some further consideration to these two positions in Chapter 3. Meanwhile, and what I have tried to suggest in this chapter, there was a third possibility—a kinship between religion and science.

We have approached this view of a kinship between religion and science, by looking at the part which intuition or disclosure plays in scientific method, when that method is seen in particular as a search for invariants such as points, force, mass, and so on. We then asked, in order to discover a distinctive reference for these invariants: where else do we find disclosures? Our answer was: in typically personal situations. And then we saw, with specific examples, the use that science makes in its methods and generalizations—whether in organic chemistry, or physics, or elsewhere—of symbols or expressions that echo personal disclosures. Science, we concluded, is at least consistent with a personal view of the universe. So, if the scientist needs to be religious, it will be because "person" is a religious category. Is it? What is man? That is our question for Chapter 2.

2

What is Man?

In Chapter 1, where I was concerned to argue for a kinship between science and religion, I concentrated on one feature of scientific method, namely its search for invariants, such as points, force, mass, atom, and so on. All these, I said, were given in disclosures; they were to be understood by reference to an intuition. In this way I tried to mediate between those who say that such invariants label "things" (when we find the world impossibly cluttered up with scientific furniture) and those who say that such invariants are only jingles (whereupon these characteristic categories of science seem to be talking about nothing at all). Mediating between those two views, I claimed that these invariants pointed to, belonged to, were to be grounded in, disclosures for which each invariant supplied its own particular route. Each invariant is linked with a series of verifiable terms which specify a route to a disclosure which fulfils them. In this way scientific invariants had a basis in fact which the second view seems to deny to them altogether, but it is a basis less rigid than the first view supposed. But where, we next asked, could we find adequate currency for what these disclosures, evoked by invariants, revealed? What were the invariants in different ways and from different directions distinctively talking about? And to answer that question we asked another: where else do we find disclosures? And the answer was: in typically personal situations. And to meet the objection that such situations seem to have no relation whatever to scientific discourse I then showed how science, in its actual methods and theorizing, made use in various ways of considerations or even phrases which echoed, or might be understood as hinting at, distinctively personal situations. So I concluded that science is at least suggestive of, and certainly quite consistent with, an understanding of the universe in personal categories. But even if science can be thus said to appeal in various ways to a model of personal interchange, that fact could have no religious significance unless something about persons eludes the net of science. What I was saying in Chapter I only gives the scientist a religious perspective if "person" proves to be a religious category. Is it? What is man? That brings me to the theme of the present chapter.

It is often claimed that developments in modern science compromise human personality. What is this threat of science to human personality? It takes both less sophisticated and more sophisticated forms, and I have selected just three of these various forms for our attention.

a. First, let us look at one of the rather less sophisticated forms which arises out of large-scale developments in physics. Here the argument runs something like this. Man might have seemed very important and very significant when he could place himself at the heart of the universe—when the earth was considered to be a cosmic centre, and man the dominant figure on the earth. Here was a picture calculated to give man cosmic significance, to spotlight his central position. Not so now. Man is an insignificant speck in a vast universe. The earth itself—let alone man—is a mere speck in a universe of vast, unfathomable distances. Of these vast distances we are reminded daily by talk about inter-stellar spaces, galaxies, projectiles passing the moon and going on for ever, and so on. Then, for good measure, there is always the medical man to add his epilogue, or perhaps, his epitaph. Man (he tells us) is a trivial organism, living a precarious existence; a few deadly germs, hitherto unknown, from another planet and he could be snuffed out for ever. Here is one of the least sophisticated versions of the scientific threat to human personality.

b. Then there is a second and rather more sophisticated form of this threat, which we will approach by a rather tortuous route. Let our journey begin from the French philosopher, Descartes, often called the father of modern philosophy. Ever since Descartes, though he was not himself the originator of the doctrine, it has been customary to talk of man being made up of two elements—a body and a soul—two elements so distinct and so different as to be virtually unrelated and unrelatable. Now the philosophical difficulties behind this view are, of course, absolutely enormous. Even Descartes recognized the appalling problem he faced on this picture to account for what has been traditionally called the interaction of body and mind.[1] Even Descartes recognized the problem, with this picture, of saying what happens when I decide to lift my arm and then do so. But Descartes was nothing if not ingenious, and he thought he had solved the difficulty by suggesting—most ingeniously— that a man's body and his mind or soul (let us not at the moment trouble about the alternative description) met at a point, at just one little, single point. A point, he considered, being un-extended could readily find a place for itself in somebody's unextended mind. Yet at the same time, a point could be seen, and much more readily perhaps, as part of an extended surface like the human body. Here then was a solution to the problem of interaction. Mind and body met, but met only in a point. Here was the junction through which all body–mind trans-actions passed. Now as a speculative solution it was ingenious enough. We might well say it deserved alpha plus plus. But when Descartes came to identify this little point as the pineal gland, and then regarded this gland mechanically as a little door turning on a central axis, through which animal spirits passed, so that the stream could press on the door (body affecting mind) or the door press on the stream (mind affecting body), his account was hardly so convincing. Perhaps it deserves no more than gamma delta. In more recent days, philosophers as different as James Ward, G. F. Stout, and lately Gilbert Ryle, have shown the inadequacy—if not absurdity—of talking about human behaviour in terms of minds and bodies (and their "interactions"), as though these were two different objects in counterpart realms. But what was a philosophical absurdity went for long unheeded, not least—and here we are moving

---

[1] Notice that this label for the problem tacitly presupposes a "mind" and "body" dualism and in its very expression creates its insolubility.

towards our main topic—because Descartes' view provided a very convenient division of labour, especially as between doctor and priest. Scientific medicine indeed thrived as it had never thrived before, when doctor and priest each got on with their respective jobs, neither bothering about the other. Each could bless Descartes for providing a *modus vivendi* for them both.

Now that is the background to such a book as F. G. Garrison's *History of Medicine*,[1] monumental in terms of weight if nothing else, which gives a full and detailed account of the development of medicine, ranging from primitive if not prehistoric times to the scientific medicine of our own day. It is highly probable, says Garrison, that "in all primitive societies, priest, magician, and medicine-man were one and the same".[2] But, he continues, "medicine could not begin to be medicine until it was dissociated from magic and religion",[3] which, with perhaps some special pleading, he puts together. It was necessary for medical development that the functions of priest, magician, and medicine man should "become specialized and differentiated".[4] And then he reflects, rather sadly, that "even today, medicine sometimes partakes of magical and mystic (religious) as well as of scientific elements".[5] If it does, Garrison would say it is something to be deplored. It is very difficult to realize that that kind of remark could pass virtually unquestioned some thirty years ago in the fourth edition of Garrison's work in 1929. It only goes to show how long science could make headway, and apparently be successful, on a background theory which is riddled with philosophical difficulties and absurdities. But by now the day of reckoning has arrived. In our own time, medicine itself has been forced to recognize the impossibility of the Cartesian dichotomy by its increasing concern with what are called psychosomatic illnesses—illnesses which cannot easily be located in either "mind" or "body", and of which perhaps

[1] Philadelphia and London, 4th edn, 1929.
[2] Op. cit., p. 23 (inserted note).
[3] Ibid.
[4] Ibid.
[5] Ibid.

(I speak as an ignorant layman) asthma is the plainest example. Physiological medicine, advancing so long with the flag of Descartes, concentrating on "bodies", is not enough. Psychosomatic illnesses have burst through Garrison's neat division of labour. Now, at first blush it might seem that this break-through would lead directly and easily to a new synthesis of science and religion, body and soul being no longer separate, but somehow forming a unity. Will not medicine, it might be said, provide in this way a new meeting-place for religion and science? Will not spiritual ministrations come to their own alongside medical ministrations? Does not medicine, especially when it is more and more concerned with psychosomatic illnesses, demand a religious view of human personality? Obviously, more than physiological medicine is wanted.

But let us not jump too hastily to conclusions. I warned us that the path to this second threat of science to religion was rather tortuous, and we are not at the end yet. For, even if medicine needs to go beyond the borders of *physiological medicine*, need it go beyond *psychological* medicine? Some years ago now I chanced to see a most disarming Ministry of Health Memorandum, which welcomed church services in hospitals but set them alongside Christmas parties and community singing, as all being important possible ways to raise morale. How lucky was the hospital with the heart-throb nurse, the debonair doctor, and the smiling priest. That worship can or should raise morale we need not doubt; but does it do no more? Here is the crucial question, and dependent on the answer comes the possibility either of further conflict or some larger synthesis of science and religion. The priest may be welcomed for no more than his cheerful smile above a bright white collar, and because the morale of the ward always soars after his visit. But perhaps the priest believes, poor chap, that he has something distinctive to contribute; well, no harm in letting him think so (some may whisper) so long as he is at least a psychological success. So, what might have been mistaken not only for an admission of the religious character of personality, but even for a positive recognition of the importance of it; what might have seemed to be an incipient victory for religion, becomes almost at once an utter and ignominious defeat. The soul may have been a puzzling concept, but it may now be reduced quite firmly to a topic for psychology and nothing more. Mind and body may be no longer pictured as a dualism; they may be rightly seen as a whole and a unity. In such ways medicine may have advanced far beyond Garrison's picture. But any hopes cherished by religion are soon shattered by realizing that there is nothing supposed to be left beyond the reach, at farthest, of psychological medicine. The tentacles of science seem, once again, to have succeeded in excluding religion. Persons may no longer be satisfactorily treated by physiological medicine—true enough—but (it is said) they need no more than the psychiatrist next door. Nothing need make its way to the manse or the rectory.

c. So we come to the third, and perhaps the most sophisticated of all contemporary scientific threats to human personality, and this arises out of the progress in calculating machines. It arises from the progress in that realm of science called cybernetics, where an attempt is made to understand human behaviour on the analogy of electrically operated calculating machines. Now there is an undoubted analogy between the human brain and the electronic calculating machine and by that I mean that the same mathematical pattern fits both. The same calculations, in other words, can be helpful, both to the brain physiologist on the one hand, and to the electronic engineer on the other. What then, says this argument, is man but a huge calculating machine? From the other side, what is a calculating machine but a very primitive man? Machines can slip up, so can men. Translation machines can even vary the translation of certain words, according to a regular pattern, more or less complex. They can thereby produce "characteristic styles" and so on. What, now, is distinctive, let alone religious, about human personality? Apparently his most characteristic behaviour (it is said) does not extend beyond what can be displayed by a calculating machine. The more complex a calculating machine, the closer it approximates to the structure of the brain, and the closer will its "performance" then resemble human behaviour.

The conclusion to these three less or more sophisticated scientific approaches to personality would seem to be that persons form no more than a topic for scientific discourse; that there is really nothing about human behaviour which eludes the treatment of science. So much for the threat to human personality.

But those three arguments are not without their counter-arguments; they are not without their consequent difficulties. To these I shall pass in turn.

a. First of all, the counter-argument against the least sophisticated of the arguments we have considered. Are we specks in a vast unfathomable universe? Of course we are, but it does *not* mean that we are devoid of cosmic significance. Size is no clue to value whatever, except possibly in the case of pigs and livestock. They may be more valuable for being big. On the contrary, a penny stamp containing the Lord's Prayer (say) written ten times is valuable for being so small. Size is no clue whatever to value or significance—some big things are very valuable, and some extremely small things are even more valuable. In fact, ever to suppose, as even some religious people have done in days past, that man's significance can be analysed in terms of size or spatial position, is to play the enemy's game. For it is to admit, as a presupposition, that the significance of man is a wholly spatio-temporal matter, and, being that, it cannot in any sense be religious. The game is up from the start. Rather let man be the speck that he is. Let him survey a vast, unfathomable universe, but notice the word: "unfathomable". The universe is so vast that man could never finish surveying it. It is not a question of the universe being very big, or very very big, or very . . . repeated 1027 times . . . big. The universe is . . . unfathomable. Man looks to himself, to the earth, to the moon, to the stars, to outer space . . . unending. But is not this the very way by which to evoke a sense of mystery? Does there not break in on us, at some point or other in this ever-expanding story, a sense of our mysterious kinship with the universe? "When I consider thy heavens, the moon and the stars, which thou hast ordained . . . the galaxies and outer space . . . what is man?"[1] And the

[1] Cf. Ps. 8.

answer is inevitably that man is a being who meets God in that mysterious fellowship which is evoked as we survey the vast unfathomable universe. If such a disclosure has not broken in on us yet, there is no need to be dispirited. For, precisely because the universe is unfathomable, there is never any need to stop our survey. On the contrary there is every need to go on and on and on and on . . . which means that there is the ever-present hope that some time, some day, at some point, the mystery will break in on us. I am reminded in this connection, of the hymn which occurred so aptly at the funeral service of Sir Arthur Eddington in Trinity College chapel, Cambridge: "The duteous day now closeth. . . ." It is a hymn[1] which speaks of something extremely close to Eddington's heart, of "all the heavenly splendour", which "breaks forth in starlight tender, from myriad worlds unknown", when "man, the marvel seeing", has "joy of beauty not his own". He is "lost in the abyss of wonder" but in being lost, he discovers heaven and himself. This is man, a speck in a vast unfathomable universe, but not lacking significance—indeed, finding his cosmic status in a cosmic wonder. Let me not claim too much. I am well aware that so far I have *proved* nothing. But I have set up a counter-argument which shows that a religious view of human personality is at any rate a live option to the first and least sophisticated of the scientific views which threaten it.

b. What, secondly, about psychosomatic medicine? Do we need more than the techniques of the medical psychiatrist? If we take a religious view of human personality, plainly we shall need more than those techniques, for the basic claim of religion is for the transcendence of man, at least in the sense that man is not exhausted by any spatio-temporal account of him. Further, if the whole man is not merely a psychosomatic unity, but such a unity as is psychosomatic, and more besides, then the "health" and "well-being" and "full existence" of a person will depend on what are called spiritual ministrations as well as the ministrations of medicine, physiological and psychological. Grace will have its place alongside penicillin, insulin, relaxation techniques,

[1] *English Hymnal*, no. 278.

33

and deep analysis. The priest will have more to offer than his bright round face and clean collar. But without developing the practical implications of these reflections which would take us too far afield and away from our main purpose, let me rather summarize, more or less in my own words, some remarks of Dr Ian Skottowe on p. 156 of his *Mental Health Handbook*. Dr Skottowe is considering at this point patients who are anxious and tense, mildly depressed and rather preoccupied. And these are his comments. It is not easy (he says) sometimes to decide whether electro-convulsive therapy (E.C.T.) is wanted or not, or whether religious ministrations and treatment might help. For example, a man with endogenous depression, Dr Skottowe comments, believing that he has committed an unpardonable sin, frequently sexual, and that God has deserted him, is likely to be more speedily relieved by E.C.T. than by religious ministrations alone. On the other hand, E.C.T. is likely to be of little avail, says Dr Skottowe, to a person whose primary trouble is religious doubt or moral conflict, especially if this arises because of prolonged contemplation of some prospective decision rather than from rumination on past misdemeanours. So it would seem that even a psychiatrist, such as Dr Skottowe, recognizes that he must at least leave room for specifically distinctive religious ministrations which cannot be covered by the techniques of scientific psychiatry, and that the former are not, nor ever will be, reducible to the latter.

c. So to my third counter-argument. How far are men like machines? Now we cannot deny, and I would never wish to deny, that the same mathematical treatment can be used and developed in relation to calculating machines on the one hand, and the human brain on the other; that to the mathematician, a brain and a calculating machine have far-reaching similarities. But exactly what follows from that fact? Sine curves, ∿, are a most useful invariant for understanding both radio transmission and the formation of waves on water ruffled by the wind. And the treatment is so far parallel that people even speak of wireless "waves". But nobody in their senses thinks that their wireless set in the study is in *every* respect the same thing as the water tank in the attic. Because [ ] is a very useful invariant

34

for comparing a ten-shilling note with a pound note, and even with a five-pound note, nobody in their senses believes that those three notes are therefore in every respect identical. Because "being over fifty years old" characterizes Bertrand Russell, the Archbishop of Canterbury, and the Pope, no one would say there is nothing to choose between any one of them. The fact that the whole truth about calculating machines needs, besides the mathematical structure they share with the human brain, qualifications proper to electronics, whereas the whole truth about the human brain needs, besides the mathematical structure it shares with calculating machines, qualifications suited to the behaviour of human beings, means that calculating machines and brains are in the last resort different. That is *not* to deny the tremendous advances in understanding human behaviour that the study of cybernetics can bring about. At the same time it *is* claiming that human behaviour is not a topic which cybernetics can *wholly* exhaust. Why have people been so silly—and it is "silly" in a very sophisticated sense—why have people been so silly as to overlook that simple point? Well, I will hazard a guess: that it is simply because they have taken a view not altogether unlike that which we criticized and rejected in Chapter 1, that invariants label and describe features, indeed the only features, of the real world. They have supposed that if a similar mathematical treatment can be given to two topics, no matter how ostensibly diverse those topics may be, e.g. brains and calculating machines, then, the two topics must, despite appearances, be "really" the same. But as G. E. Moore once said, when somebody tells us that x is really y, we have the best reason for believing it is nothing of the sort. Those who make men and machines equal are like those who, in an earlier day, allowed objects to have shapes, but not "really" colour. Why? Because, they said, we have a mathematical treatment—geometry—for shape, but we have no mathematical treatment of colour. Therefore, they concluded, odd as it might seem, that colours did not "really" exist. They were "silly" in the learned philosophical sense.[1] Well, the answer to such sophistication is

[1] Cf. C. D. Broad, *The Mind and its Place in Nature* (1925), pp. 5f, who first introduced this concept of the "silly".

quite simple: just open your eyes and look. That is indeed one answer we can give to this third **argument**: look at the calculating machine and look at the fellow that runs it, and notice (as I hope you will) significant differences.

Perhaps I should remark, in rounding off this section, that I have altogether left out of account arguments that are based on the fact that each and every machine demands at least one human being distinctly different from them all; or on the fact that no one has yet found a machine falling in love with him, though some men may have found machines grand things to live with. For while I think all such arguments are very convincing in the long run, it is a long run and not a short one, and it is a longer run than I have space for in this chapter. But at least I may remark that in the end all these arguments appeal to a first-person *subjectivity* of which each of us is aware in himself and which, as subjectivity, is irreducible to third-person objects, which indeed all presuppose it. In other words, all the stories of cybernetics presuppose at least one subject about whom they are never—logically never—adequate. This is a point to which I return presently.[1]

What have I done then? So far I have tried to show that, despite the heavy batteries which were brought up against human personality, the citadel still stands. A religious view of personality is still a live option. We can even make counterattacks. Meanwhile, as I said earlier, views which would erode the religious concept of personality have not only to face counter-arguments, they have to face consequent difficulties as well, and to these we now turn. Let us look at the difficulties which a denial of the significance of human personality brings with it.

If human personality is *completely* tractable in scientific terms, there are certain serious consequences that, paradoxically enough, contemporary social scientists are the first to point out.[2]

---

[1] It is also the point which more than any other lies behind my answers to Mr Dorling's searching questions in the Supplementary Note which follows this chapter, and where I take a little further the issues raised in the lecture.

[2] See e.g. the reference to Barbara Wootton below, p. 45f.

Let me summarize just two of these difficulties, which those who deny the religious view of human personality must face, and face squarely.

a. First, there seems to be no room left for the concept of responsibility. Mrs A lifts nylons at the local store and is pleased to find herself called a kleptomaniac. Mr B commits a foul murder but it is all a matter of his blood-sugar. No need for confessions—just cases for the psychiatrist or biochemist. The psychiatrist, indeed, rather than the presbyter, is the old priest writ large. No longer are we like sheep going astray; or rather both sheep and human beings only go astray when their bio-chemistry and psycho-pathology go haywire. Let me quote part of a letter which I once had[1] from another psychiatrist, Dr Christopher Ounsted, and which I have his permission to quote. Go back to Mr B. Suppose there is a murder. "The psychiatrist, as a scientist," says Dr Ounsted, "seeks to understand the murder in causal terms. He looks for the aetiology of the crime in the murderer's genetics, in his psycho-pathology, in his blood sugar, in the electrical pulsations of his brain. He establishes a medical diagnosis: the murderer has schizophrenia or a depression." "But", continues Dr Ounsted, "when he presents to the court his analysis and diagnosis, he does not answer the one critical, though unspoken question: 'Could the murderer have chosen to let his victim live?'" But there is one question which is explicit and will certainly be asked. In relation to the McNaughton Rules, the question will be put: "Did he at the time of committing the act, labour under such a defect of reason as not to know the nature and quality of the act he was doing, or if he did know this, did he know that what he was doing was wrong?" Dr Ounsted comments: "A scientist cannot properly answer either of these questions, the unspoken one or the McNaughton question, for the language in which they are couched implies metaphysical assumptions, in principle untestable by scientific method." But Dr Ounsted is not willing to leave the matter there and he continues: "Does the scientist refuse to answer? His response will depend on the rôle in which

[1] November 1959.

37

he sees himself. He has two rôles, and must ordinarily play both simultaneously. As a scientist he must disregard free will; as a clinician he must constantly assert its claims. His daily work involves judgements such as 'this patient has regained volition and his legal status must be changed'; or 'this patient lacks the ability to make his will—he has no testamentary capacity'; or 'this patient, untreated, cannot choose but kill himself. He must be certified.' In fact," continues Dr Ounsted, "the whole purpose of medical treatment is to restore the patient to a condition in which he may make choices freely. So the psychiatrist, more than most men, is torn both ways. If he is moderate and a humble man this is all to the good." But suppose he is a scientific fanatic or bigot. He will not be torn two ways at all. And then it will happen that law and morality are excluded from his considerations, and there is then spotlighted an immense conflict between the twin foundations of modern society, law and science. Must a scientific society become amoral? With no religious view of personality, that seems to be the inevitable conclusion.

  b. The second difficulty which a denial of the religious view of personality has to face is less general, but it touches each of us rather more personally. If human personality is wholly tractable in scientific terms, if persons can be given an exhaustive scientific assessment, not only responsibility, but individuality, eccentricity, the "odd man out", cannot be tolerated. Persons become people, averages, "bods". In education, for example, the deviationist is suspect. Let me give you a very simple illustration. It happened that at a certain school half a dozen children were being tested for entrance at a time before they could either read of write. One of the methods was to put a diagram, part of which was deliberately obliterated like this, before the children:

and to ask: What is this? Five out of the six children said "a teapot", and they gained admission. One said, "I do not know", and she failed. But when the unsuccessful child arrived home she made a very significant comment. "Why didn't you say it was a teapot?" said her mother, to which the child replied, "It can't be a teapot because no one pours tea out of a thing like that." But she had failed and the others had passed. She indeed was the odd man out, eccentric, the deviationist. Yet there might well have been far more possibility in that child than in some of the five who passed. The story is a crude indication of the way in which a rigorously standardized treatment of personality might affect education. I will not enter on such hotly debated topics as that of the "eleven plus" intelligence tests. I have rather kept to less controversial ground with the teapot. But the point is the same: the more standardized educational tests become, the more will distinctiveness in personality be at a discount.

So far we have seen the challenge of contemporary science to human personality, and we have surveyed some counter-arguments which make a religious view of personality still a live option. Subsequently we have seen some difficulties which arise for our social life and culture if the scientific view is taken as the whole truth. We are indeed, in a way, back where we started. What is man? What is a person? It was Dr Ounsted, you remember, who reminded us that his difficulties involved in the end metaphysical speculation.

So to answer this question, What is man?, let us try putting it to the philosopher. Let us begin some philosophical reflections with two sentences: (1) "I'm dancing rock and roll" said by A who is doing the dancing. (2) "He's dancing rock and roll", said by B, a spectator of A. A, in uttering (1) describes something. If you say, "But in what circumstances would anyone ever say, 'I'm dancing rock and roll'?"—well, suppose someone thought that he would never dance again, but, cured of polio, he goes back to the dance floor. That is the sort of circumstance in which the first sentence might be uttered. A might say to himself, "Fancy, I'm dancing rock and roll again after all." B, who is sitting it out with a friend, comments to the friend, "He's dancing rock and roll." This is said by B of A and, again, plainly it describes something. Further, there is much, very much in common between the two assertions (1) and (2). But notice that (2) relates to nothing but what are technically "objects"; it talks of nothing but public, observable behaviour, such as that which scientific techniques will elaborate and develop. Nor is there any limit whatever to be set to this kind of scientific coverage. What will the man with an eye to dynamics mean by "He's dancing"? Answer: "He is moving in such and such directions, with such and such velocity." He will talk to us about energy and impulses, about coefficients of friction and so on. What will the medical man mean by "He's dancing rock and roll"? This time it is a story about the muscles pulling, the brain potentials taking their various values, and so on. The economist with a scientific turn will say: "Ah, here's a wage-earner, who has no money for fuel because production and transport costs are these days so high. Here is someone compelled, on Marxist grounds, to dance to get warm." This is what "He's dancing" signifies for such an economist: a long story in terms of "objects"; and this time the "objects" are such as: the marketing of coal, retail price index, production rates, labour–management relations, and so on. The psychiatrist will say: "He's dancing. Yes, he is just trying to spite Jim and Alice who are now sitting out." The anthropologist of a scientific turn will say: "Ah, yes, that's a reversion to tribal behaviour such as I saw when I went into darkest Africa." "Dancing rock and roll" can display such diversities of meaning; this is what the phrase "means" in the different contexts. Nor is there any limit to it. The mathematician, the doctor, the economist, the psychiatrist, the anthropologist, all these could continue, all night and the next day as well, the story of what "He's dancing" means. Scientific explanation and explication can continue without limit. But no matter *how many* of these stories are told, no matter *how far* these stories are developed, they will *never* talk about all that A talks about when A says to himself, "I'm dancing". No number of assertions like (2)—no matter how many—can be logically equivalent to an assertion of brand (1). Why? Well, if A were so describable without residue in terms of assertions of brand (2), A would be no more than a pattern of "objects" and the subject–object distinction would be lost. We should indeed have objectified the subject, and the very basis of all our language, of all our talking, the basic presupposition of experience itself, would have disappeared. But why, you may ask, is anyone so silly as to suppose that we could completely exhaust (1) in terms of the kind of scientific tales we can tell, rightly tell, and use-fully tell, about (2)? Why are people once again being, from the philosophical point of view, so "silly"?

I suggest there are two reasons:

a. People may have supposed that the subject–predicate form of an assertion necessarily preserves the subject–object distinc-tion. People may have supposed that because we have a "he" doing something or other, the subject–object distinction is pre-served, just as it is with "I" doing something or other. But in fact the subject–object distinction is not preserved even though a third-person assertion is in subject–predicate form. In this sense, it is an incomplete assertion, for it is an assertion com-pletely in terms of objects. "He's dancing rock and roll" has a subject–predicate form all right, but it relates wholly to objects, and the subject has disappeared. That, I suggest, is the first reason why people have made the silly claims they have for the coverage of science. They have supposed that with a subject-predicate form, the subject must be preserved. But in fact a minute's reflection shows that in some cases, and in most cases of third-person assertions, it is not.

b. So to the second reason why people have confounded the logical status of assertions (1) and (2). It has arisen, if I may sug-gest another possibility, because of a parallel which arises at a second move. Suppose somebody asks A and B, "What were you muttering just now?" Then A can say (3), "I said *'I'm dancing rock and roll'* ", and B can say (4), "I said *'He's dancing rock and roll'* ". Now these "enclosed", italicized assertions, referring back to past events, do indeed possess the same logical status, but "I" in (3) is no longer what it was. "I" is no longer the "I" that it was when, so to say, it was outside the bracket. *That* "I" has gone over to the extreme left in (3). The other "I" indeed is the "me" of a moment ago. This "I", inside the second inverted commas, is my scientific counterpart, and it is no more and no less accessible to me than to any scientist. Now simply because, when it becomes an object of reflection, (1) becomes in principle equivalent to (2), people may have supposed that the moment (1) and (2) were originally uttered, the two assertions meant the same. But they did not. For the moment after we

41

have given utterance to an assertion specifying our activity now, that activity becomes frozen; it becomes just as accessible to a scientist as to me—in fact, it is more accessible to him because he is the expert. We are more accessible to mathematicians, doctors, economists, and so on than we are to ourselves because they are the experts.

Now, what does this imply about becoming aware of ourselves, of our personality? How do we become aware of our characteristic subjectivity? Well, we simply begin where everybody must begin—with those terms which David Hume, the eighteenth-century philosopher, called "distinct perceptions", particular events frozen, so to say, from times past. We survey these as I suggested we surveyed (say) the dots in Chapter 1. We survey "distinct perceptions" until a disclosure occurs. At that point, at that particular instant, we then become aware of ourselves. What "I" means breaks in on us as we survey in this way what Hume called "a train of distinct perceptions". We look over a sequence of distinct perceptions and we come to know ourselves. It is in such a disclosure that we are aware of "I" along with, but more than, any and all of its scientific counterparts.

If this is rather puzzling let me give you an example that will be familiar to you all: David and Nathan from 2 Samuel 12. Notice the technique. Nathan tells David a story which David understands—as a spectator—in terms of "objects". There are two men, the one rich, the other poor. The rich man had many flocks and herds, the poor man had nothing, except one little ewe lamb. Unexpected visitors arrive, and the rich man's wife is "on the spot". She spares to take of her husband's flock, for whatever reason we can only invent, and sends to the poor man for his little lamb, etc.—a story perfectly coined in terms of objects. David understands it—he builds up the object picture, and he makes an impersonal judgement on it as though he were Mr Justice David sitting in the Queen's Bench division. "That man must surely die." Here is something all very impersonal—scientific and legal. But then Nathan challenges David, "Thou art the man", and the penny drops—there is a disclosure indeed. David surveys his distinct perceptions—on the one hand the

42

lamb, the two men, the guests and so on and, alongside this, the picture of Bathsheba and Uriah's death . . . and—he comes to himself. For the first time in that story he has "self-knowledge"; he knows "I". And there arise out of that story two further points. First, notice how religious language becomes at once appropriate. "Thus saith the Lord, the God of Israel" is the language that introduces suitable currency for what was disclosed when indeed the penny dropped. Secondly, for our present purpose it is even more important to notice that *David's awareness of himself subjectively is given along with the discernment objectively of a moral challenge*. Here we come to what we might even dare to call the full flowering of the picture I have tried to develop. Here we have a disclosure situation whose understanding demands everything that any and every scientific account can give, yet which *also goes further* and demands a distinctive concept of human personality, one which arises alongside and together with a concept of moral obligation and responsibility. Such a personal disclosure is thus a situation which *subjectively* transcends the spatio-temporal and assures us of our religious individuality; and *objectively* it appears as a moral challenge to which we answer, to which we make an appropriate response, as and when we exercise our responsibility. The broad conclusion is that personality is a religious category when it is revealed to each of us in such a disclosure. It is thus the topic of any and all scientific talk about "me"; but it is more distinctively a topic which such discourse never—and it is a logical "never"—exhausts. Here is a concept of personality, which can allow for and welcome the full and ever-expanding range of scientific inquiry; it can also help bridge the yawning gulf in our civilization between the scientific and the moral, for it is a concept rooted in and common to both types of discourse. So the religious man welcomes science in so far as it provides more and more occasions for exercising responsible behaviour, more and more occasions for uniting science and morality within his religious vision.

And what is the corollary to all this? When in this way we associate together, in a religious vision, personality, moral responsibility, and scientific development, it follows that it is

to a religious vision we must turn if we wish to grapple successfully with the vital problems of our time, of which I select but
three, and mention each extremely briefly.

a. The first we might call "bombs and genetics". Lord
Adrian, in a recent Fawley lecture,[1] argued that what aroused
genuine concern over atom bomb tests was not so much the
prospect of their results being used in war as that the resulting
increase in radiation due to such tests would be likely to cause
an increase in congenital disorders in future generations. He also
added that at present, through the medical use of X-rays, the
human gonads were being exposed to a level of radiation more
than twenty times as great as that due to bomb tests. Yet there
could be no doubt, he continued, of the beneficial effects of
X-rays. Their lethal effect had been turned to good use for
killing cells over whose growth the human body had lost
control. But there was another and less obvious risk to be faced.
It had been found that mutations could be induced in Droso-
phila by an exposure to X-rays well below that needed to cause
obvious cell damage. Mutations are usually harmful and we
cannot be sure that even with our routine examinations of the
chest the total gonadal exposure does not lead occasionally to
the birth of a defective child and adds slightly to the incidence
of leukaemia. Here is the start of a far-reaching moral problem.
How far ought we continue to make use of X-ray examination
and diagnosis? How far ought we to take risks over atomic
fall-out? Here are moral problems indeed and I submit it is only
when men are not only scientific but also religious that they
will have both the information and the moral stimulus and
discernment by which to solve them.

b. The second problem, or group of problems, arises out of
technological development. It is typical of technology that, of
all the sciences, it is the most distinctively impersonal. The
slide-rule typifies it. We just "read off" the answer. There need
be no disclosure, no intuition. At the same time, technology

---

[1] *The Risks of Progress* (University of Southampton, 1960), published
in an abbreviated form in the magazine *Esso*, Winter 1959–60, pp. 8–9,
from which, with only minor alterations, the next seven sentences are
quoted.

raises a host of moral problems, from automation to problems of general culture—more problems, I dare to say, than any other branch of any science. But I suggest to you that herein lies the very salvation of technology, for these moral problems emphasize that technology—even technology, especially technology—can be, needs to be, and must be comprised within the religious vision, as a condition of their satisfactory solution. The very problems technology raises contain the seeds of its cultural fulfilment and its religious salvation.

c. Thirdly, let us turn again to the psychiatrist. The problem here has been already raised in Dr Ounsted's letter. That the moralist needs to supplement the psychiatrist is plain.[1] To take only a chance quotation from D. H. Stott in a report, *Delinquency and Human Nature*, sponsored by the Carnegie United Kingdom Trust:[2] "So it seems to me", reflects Stott after an immense research project, "that the moralist and the psychologist can eat grass together. Society must say to the individual that he is responsible for his actions and hold him to account for them. In our approved school work, however deep a lad's emotional disturbance, the staff and the psychologist must point out to him that, much as we understand his difficulties and their origin, the public and the law cannot be expected to accept any such excuses or mitigations, that it is up to him to pull himself together." "In our present society", concludes Stott, "we cannot afford the luxury of endlessly tolerating neurotic ways of life, delinquent or otherwise." Or again, Dr Barbara Wootton, in her book *Social Science and Social Pathology* (1959) argues that the erosion of morality by science is only dangerous when it is thought that science is a *substitute* for morality. I need hardly note in parenthesis that Dr Barbara Wootton is no heavily committed Christian, and it is all the more significant that she says

[1] That we must preserve a diversity of explanations—moral and psychological—is also the conclusion reached on philosophical grounds in the psychological study of motives in *The Concept of Motivation*, by R. S. Peters (1958). The same point is also made about the relations of social science and theology within a Christian sociology by Professor T. S. Simey in *The Concept of Love in Child Care* (1960), e.g. on p. 68 and in ch. 9.

[2] Op cit., p. 375.

this. "Refocusing attention away from culpability and responsibility and towards choice of treatment", Lady Wootton argues with cogency, "in no way involves indifference to or rejection of moral consideration: that choice itself must be conditioned by moral factors."[1] Only when this is forgotten does the "intrusion"[2] of medicine into the sphere of morality become alarming. On all sides then it is granted that the moralist and the psychologist are *both* needed: as we noted earlier, room must be found for both in any endeavour to improve man or society. What we now further claim is that a justification of this *modus vivendi* is possible, and perhaps is only possible, on the basis of a religious view of personality; and that such a view is a *sine qua non* if we would grapple reasonably with these problems of our contemporary civilization. For I have argued that it is on a religious view of personality and within a religious vision that a scientific account of personality and an account of personality as morally responsible are held together. It is on a religious view that we find the necessary links between the scientific language of psychiatry and the language of moral responsibility, just as we shall argue in the next chapter that religious language also supplies an answer to a not dissimilar logical problem in another

[1] Op. cit., p. 253. The whole of ch. 8 ("Mental Disorder and Criminal Responsibility") is relevant and important. Cf. a remark by Lady Wootton a little later: Only when we remove "the presumption of responsibility" can science "pursue unhindered its morally neutral task of designing . . . a method of achieving a prescribed aim that is most likely to be effective; but whether that instrument be hydrogen bomb, hangman's noose, or analyst's couch, the demonstration of effectiveness is not and cannot be, by itself, a command to use" (p. 254). The implication is that what is needed is *both* science *and* morality.

[2] Ibid., p. 338. On p. 339 Lady Wootton notes: "The struggle between the rival merits of medicine and morality seems to have become the contemporary equivalent of the 19th century battle between scientific and religious explanations of cosmic events or of terrestrial evolution." What I argue in fact is that this time religion can be a reconciler in the battle, provided that it learns lessons from its own conflicts, not least the lesson that there may be many logical treatments of the same situation. The problem is not that of dispensing with every explanation except one; but rather the problem of how to combine, if possible, these diverse logical approaches to the same situation. This problem I face in Chapter 3.

field, the problem of scientific fragmentation—how, if possible, to combine scientific languages which are logically diverse.

Allow me at the end to guard against a possible misunderstanding. I always see my position as that of a frontiersman facing the pagan rather more than the believer, and that means that at this point I overhear someone saying: "Do you really think that religious practices will be as important as all that? Do not statistics show that religious people are no better than others —perhaps even worse—at keeping themselves out of the police courts?" Well, here is material indeed for argument. On the one hand, I remember that in Michael Argyle's statistical survey of religious behaviour,[1] he shows that boys at least in Glasgow who attend churches are less delinquent than boys who do not. But on the other hand I am bound to admit that sometimes it seems as though the profession of visible religious practices is no clue whatever to the moral stamina of the people who profess them. Yet in any case, let us notice, my argument is not that religious *practices*, as such, will save civilization. What I am arguing is that religious *vision* will, and it is a sobering and humiliating thought that our practice does but rarely equal our vision.

Now for a brief summary of the argument of this chapter. First, we looked at just three of the threats to human personality which seem to arise from developments in modern science. The vast perspectives of physics seems to make man a mere speck in the universe. The development of psychological medicine, the recognition of psychosomatic illnesses, which might have been thought to do more justice to the wholeness of man's spiritual personality, may in the end be only the more devastating in their implications, when the psychiatrist is thought to replace the priest. Again, since both the human brain and the electronic calculating machine are mathematically congruous, are not men just machines? And yet, as we saw, these arguments have their counter-arguments. The vastness of the universe can evoke a disclosure of mystery. Secondly, even the psychiatrist can leave room for religious ministrations. Thirdly, men are no more

[1] See his *Religious Behaviour* (1958), p. 97.

47

wholly machines, because of certain resemblances, than Earl Russell is the Archbishop of Canterbury because of certain similarities. Further, not only have the arguments such counter-arguments; they raise in themselves difficult problems in relation to man's freedom and responsibility, far-reaching problems for our social life and culture.

What is man? Our answer is that man is what each of us finds himself to be when a disclosure occurs such as Nathan evoked for David. Man there finds himself to be scientific *and more*, in a religious disclosure whereby and wherein he also becomes aware objectively of a moral challenge. So it is to a religious vision, maybe regretfully contrasted with practices, that we must turn if we wish to grapple successfully with such vital topics of our time as are both moral and scientific, and which raise those challenging questions which cluster around atomic tests and genetics, technological developments, and psychiatry and the law.

In Chapters 1 and 2 I have argued for the kinship of science and religion, and the benefits to civilization which a recognition of that kinship can bring. But let us not be self-satisfied. Are there not features of scientific method which make science necessarily irreligious? That is the question we face in the next chapter. Dare a scientist risk being religious?

MEN AND MACHINES

I HAVE explained earlier[1] how the following papers came to be written. Mr Dorling's frank and forthright presentation of the problem comes first, and is followed by my answers to the specific questions he formulates.

The Problem, as Introduced by Mr Dorling

The kind of psychology which I am studying is not particularly interested in "introspection", is not particularly interested even in "the mind". The reasons are quite simple: introspection has not led to results which are particularly intelligible, or sufficiently reliable—they depend far too much on the theoretical views of the person who introspects; the mind is an entity we do not mention because we are not sure what anybody means by "the mind"—the phrase may have several different meanings, and we find that the use of this particular term tends to obscure our problems rather than to clarify them.

We are much more interested in the behaviour of humans and of animals, and in trying to discover the mechanisms underlying such behaviour. Our work is closely related to that of the physiologist. The chief differences are, first, that the behaviour we study is usually much more complex than the behaviour he is able to study with his present techniques; secondly, he tries to find out about the mechanisms underlying behaviour, usually by smashing up the machine that displays them, e.g. by cutting pieces off the brain and seeing what happens, while we find that at any rate for the complex levels of behaviour we are interested in, this method where it has proved practicable has not proved very fruitful and that in many cases, particularly in work with human beings, it is obviously quite impracticable.

Our method is to study the behaviour first, then to build

[1] See Preface, p. vii.

hypotheses about the kind of mechanism which we think might underlie the behaviour in question, to derive predictions from these hypotheses, and then, by observing behaviour in specially contrived situations, to attempt to confirm or falsify our hypotheses about the underlying mechanisms.

There are two related assumptions which the majority, or at any rate a very powerful minority, of workers in this field make, and which certainly seem to run counter to traditional Christian views.

a. That if we knew enough about the brain we would, in principle, be able to explain completely human behaviour and human experience.

b. That in principle there is no aspect of human behaviour that could not be duplicated by an appropriately designed machine.

These statements raise serious problems both for our ordinary ways of thinking about human beings, and for the Christian view of people. I shall put to Professor Ramsey half a dozen more specific questions related to this problem as it touches: the brain, free will, purposes and intentions, consciousness, human feelings and emotions, and the duplication of human behaviour by machines.

1. We have known for a long time that there must be a very close relationship between what happens in the brain and our behaviour and experiences, but until recently we have had little information on the details of this relationship, particularly as it touches the higher mental functions. But we may not have to remain in the dark for very much longer. I will mention three lines of evidence which suggest this:

If we stimulate electrically the temporal lobes of the brain in conscious patients we get the most vivid and detailed memory reports. The patient describes accurately, as if it were happening at the time, an experience that may have happened five, ten, or twenty years before. For example, the words of a song which the patient cannot have heard for many years may be repeated faithfully with the comment, "It is as if I were hearing him singing it now."

Secondly, I mention a study which originally began with rats. It was found that if electrodes were implanted in appropriate sites in the brain of a rat, and if the rat were permitted to stimulate itself electrically by repeatedly pressing a bar with its feet, it would continue to do so for rates as high as five thousand presses an hour, and for as long as it could go on doing so before physical exhaustion supervened, perhaps for as long as forty-eight hours. And with electrodes in appropriate sites these rats would learn mazes or cross electrified grids in order to stimulate themselves.

Turning to humans, we have now found that there are analogous sites in their brains where, if a subject is stimulated, he will describe the experience he gets as extremely pleasant and will plead with the doctor to continue stimulating.

Thirdly, I remind you of the now well-known operation of frontal leucotomy. The behaviour of a patient after his frontal lobes have been removed differs significantly from his previous behaviour, in so far as he has now a tendency, after the operation, to be governed by momentary impulses rather than by long-term aims, and a tendency to ignore social conventions of etiquette or of morality in order to satisfy his immediate more-or-less-primitive desires. One of the things which seems to be cut off when the frontal lobes are cut off is the individual's conscience.

What I want to ask Professor Ramsey is whether he thinks the Christian has any reason to be worried by the implications of these kinds of discovery or by the thought of such discoveries of this kind as the future may bring?

2. Those who hold to the two assumptions that I mentioned earlier, have to suppose that our experience of free will is compatible with determinism. Their chief argument is that, when we say we have free will, surely we are not denying that our choices are governed by, for instance, our beliefs and attitudes? Surely we are not meaning to assert that they are literally un-caused? If we assert this, would we not have to assert that the particles that the physicist studies are much better candidates for possessing free will than you or I? I know this is a very controversial issue, and that highly intelligent people have taken

both sides on the question; what I want to ask Professor Ramsey is, does he think that a Christian is, as a Christian, more or less bound to take one side in the dispute?

3. The production of guided missiles was the first serious challenge to the conventional belief that purposes and intentions are the prerogative of human beings and cannot be displayed by machines. I admit that there is still a big gap between these simple mechanisms and genuine purpose or intention. Nevertheless we now have machines (for example a robot that "learns" a maze and takes short cuts when they are offered) that display behaviour which, if we saw it in an animal or in a child, we would naturally describe as purposive or governed by intentions; and those who design such machines certainly suppose that they are constructing mechanisms, at least analogous to those in the brain, which actually do control simple forms of human and animal behaviour. Does Professor Ramsey consider that the Christian is bound as a Christian to oppose this view, or does he think that a Christian may freely take one side or the other on this issue?

4. Next, I want to suggest that "consciousness"—whatever that is—is not something which could not in principle be shown in a machine. Certainly, a large number of psychologists (and even a few normal people as well) hold this apparently paradoxical view. They would say that the word "conscious" has many different uses but that any of these uses could in principle be applied to an appropriate machine. For example, when we say that a person is unconscious, we mean simply that he is not reacting normally to stimuli, both in the sense that he is not making gross observable reactions at the time and in the sense that he is not laying down memory traces that will be utilizable later. Now we only need a machine with differential reactions to stimuli and with some kind of memory mechanism, for *this* distinction between "conscious" and "unconscious" to apply to it. Take another example: when I say, "I am now conscious of my heart-beats" do I mean much more than the following:
   a. That I am now able to say 'tum-tum-tum' in time with them.

b. That I am now able on demand to describe their characteristic changes in intensity.

c. That I am able on demand to compare and contrast them with other familiar feelings such as throbbing pains or dull repetitive sounds.

d. That so long as I am concentrating my attention on being ready to make any of these reactions, I am relatively oblivious to other stimuli that may impinge on my sense-organs.

Now, provided we can design a robot that would have some semblance to the use of a language (though this itself is a fascinatingly difficult problem), there would be no essential difficulty in designing one with which we could make *this* distinction between "being conscious of *x*" and "not being conscious of *x*".

There are those who still insist that consciousness is an unanalysable something and that therefore any attempt to say what we mean by it in particular cases is misguided. Defenders of the view I am presenting will usually ridicule such people by asking some such question as, "Well, have you any reason then to suppose that this mysterious something is possessed by anyone other than yourself?"—a question that is traditionally unanswerable.

Of course I do not want to say that anyone has yet *given* an adequate explanation of consciousness; I am only saying that many psychologists and philosophers interested in psychology think that this problem will eventually be solved. Does the Christian have to say no? What does Professor Ramsey think?

5. *Human feelings and emotions.* I do not think it will be so *very* difficult to design machines that will show the more animal emotions: rage, fear, excitement, desire, but it is going to be a much more difficult problem to design one that would show the more specifically human feelings, e.g. that would feel humility, or remorse, or spiritual uplift.

At this level we should have to build into our machine such things as long-term aims and beliefs. The latter, for instance, might be done in the following way: a machine would be said to believe a statement if it answered in the affirmative when it was asked whether it believed it or not, and if it behaved in a way that could plainly only be regarded as intelligently adaptive on the assumption that the statement believed was in fact true.

Of course, problems of this order of complexity have so far hardly been considered, even by psychologists and philosophers; perhaps they assume that once the simpler problems have been solved these will prove easy enough; perhaps on the other hand they feel at the moment still very uncertain of their ability ever to solve them. Does a Christian have to discourage them; does he have to say that they will never be able to talk adequately of such human feelings and emotions in language that could be applied equally well to a machine?

6. I want to remind you that while the statements I have been presenting are in one sense wild speculations, they are at the same time definite implications of the assumptions that underlie much of the thinking of many contemporary psychologists. The Christian must either try to reconcile the view of human nature that I have outlined with the Christian view, if this be possible (and I remind you that at heart the psychologist is not trying to explain away, but simply to explain), or he has to tell psychologists how they ought to change their present working assumptions. It is going to do no good just laughing at them or saying that they are fantastic. It is part of the history of science that scientists spend much of their time trying to solve problems that philosophers and theologians tell them are unsolvable: Newton asked almost blasphemously, "Why do the heavenly bodies revolve in the way they do?" Darwin was not content merely to describe the differences between the different species, but insisted on asking, in the face of the laughter of the theologians, how these differences arose. Laughing at the hopes of the scientist has proved far too dangerous in the past to be worth trying again. The problem raised by contemporary psychological assumptions and hopes must be faced up to. So to my last question.

We have all heard of chess-playing machines, and most of us have heard of translating machines. To-day some mathematical physicists use a machine which analyses a batch of physical data, guesses, one after another, at equations that might fit these data, and successively tests the equations for goodness-of-fit. This machine is doing something very like what the physicist himself does when he invents a new hypothesis. Where do we go from here? I do not think it would be impossible to programme a machine to perform such a task as making a précis. Admittedly the verse hitherto produced by machines has been reported to have been of inferior quality.

But how does Professor Ramsey react to the suggestion that it may not be very long now before we have a machine that will deliver a sermon?

Comments on the Questions Mr Dorling Raises

(1) Has the Christian any reason to be worried by the implications for human behaviour of the electrical stimulation of memory or pleasure sensations, by frontal leucotomy and the like?

Some Christians, I fear, like Wilberforce in days past, might wish to take a desperate stand in terms of some such categorical assertion of supposed fact as "rock pigeons are what rock pigeons have always been". In our own day this might become "human nature will always be what human nature is", rather implying that the full extension of these scientific experiments to human behaviour has to be ruled out as impossible. But that position seems to me not only to indicate a shocking lack of imagination but to be even more disastrously a disingenuous counsel of despair. That memory may be improved beyond all expectation; that pleasure sensations may be stimulated at will; that frontal leucotomy may lead to a zest for life which sits loose to all convention—all this, let no one deny. But we may recall a significant remark which Mr Dorling made in the course of his exposition. Suppose the patient pleads with the doctor to continue his pleasure stimulation. Does the doctor continue, or does he not? Some of the rats who repeated the stimuli too often collapsed from sheer exhaustion and died. In short, these far-reaching developments only increase the need for moral decision and raise moral issues in relatively unknown and novel situations, e.g. should memory be improved if such improvement is to be gained at the expense of other features of a man's mental health? Ought X to be made happier, and when, and for how long? Shall Y satisfy, uninhibited, his more or less primitive desires?

Who is to decide these questions, and on what grounds? That is the only implication that need worry us, and I should have thought it ought to worry everybody, Christian or not. But that reflection does not end my discussion of this question.

Let me open up another avenue like this. Let us ask ourselves: Does the person after frontal leucotomy lose *all* moral insight? Does he lose altogether his conscience? At any rate, if he does, have we not then the responsibility of re-educating him morally? Suppose, for example, that after frontal leucotomy a person with a zest for life which sits loose to all convention, rapes a young girl or beats up a harmless pedestrian; surely our accounting for the fact in terms of frontal leucotomy does not relieve us from a responsibility for the man's moral re-education; nor from our judgement that his behaviour is morally evil—though he is not responsible for it and may well not be blameworthy.

There is yet another line of reasoning we may develop in relation to this question. In one way these developments in human physiology raise no more difficulties for the philosopher than might be raised by striking changes in a man's environment. In any case, the fact that scientific knowledge is probing more and more behind the temporary wall of our bodies is no new event. But it does not alter my personality *at least in this fundamental sense*, viz. I do not feel less "myself" because I have lost my limbs, had a lung collapse, or a frontal leucotomy performed. Suppose, however, it might be argued, I was to all appearances "completely" changed. Well, I suppose there have been such cases, e.g. cases of multiple personality such as that of Sally Beauchamp or even Dr Jekyll and Mr Hyde. But in such circumstances—of completely different behaviour characteristics—it is *not* logically impossible to say "I am A and B". Certainly the religious man will be prepared to say that; he can and does readily allow for, and indeed explicitly provide for, the whole of a man's behaviour given by scientific stories not being *the whole* story. This in fact is the claim for immortality. So the residual question which arises from the first challenge seems to be this: Is personality—or is it not—*wholly* in principle tractable by science?

(2) *When we talk of free will, do we mean that acts of will are literally uncaused?*

The question is crucial because only then is it difficult to hold both a belief in determinism and in free will, which it does seem (I agree) that many psychologists wish to do, and which indeed the kind of answer I have given to question (1) implies.

There are two reflections worth making:

a. First of all, a negative point. To talk about "acts of will" being either "caused" or "uncaused" seems to me a logical blunder—rather like asking what is the square root of my singing. To talk of an "act of will" does not (I suggest) name an event in space and time. That it has some sort of reference to spatio-temporal events and to observable behaviour, we need neither doubt nor deny. But what we assert is that an "act of will" is an ontological peculiar which, while displaying itself in spatio-temporal behaviour, is not limited to the behaviour it displays in this way.

b. What "more", then, is there in an "act of will" than the spatio-temporal behaviour associated with it?

To believe in "free will" is to believe that in certain cases of decision—whose ancestry may be more and more revealed, at least once the decision is "taken", by scientific inquiry—in certain cases of decision, at the moment of decision, we know ourselves active in a way which transcends all that a scientific story, however complex, might talk of. On what grounds do we make this claim? Well, consider the alternative. On the alternative, our behaviour is wholly a matter of "objects" and thus we have committed the *logical blunder* of objectifying the subject.[1] Or—another point—look at those who have tried to account for what each of us knows himself to be in terms of

[1] See pp. 40f. above.

57

"objects". What then becomes of self-identity? It was in relation to this question, we may remember, that Hume had to confess that his effort to account for the self in terms of objects was a failure.

3. *What of the machines that learn how to find their way through a maze, even take short cuts, and so on? What of guided missiles? Does it mean that machines can display purposiveness?*

Let it be said that we normally take certain patterns to be distinctive of personality. Perhaps we never make such an inference in the matter of a very simple pattern, and I seem to remember that there even is a mathematical theory of mazes for which it would be very easy to programme a machine. Guided missiles, too, have a movement which is completely describable in mathematical terms which are sufficiently complex. In such cases we might well find no need for any "further" explanation.

But the question is: *Is* this the case, *could* this and no more be the case, with a "person"? Admittedly, sometimes we now see a pattern of stones on a beach, and seeing them as though they had been arranged purposively, we may deduce the work of a person—and we may be wrong. But our inference may be more reliable if the pattern is the more complicated—though here again it may be wrong. But when we use "right" and "wrong" in these instances is it merely a description of a more complicated pattern than less, which has arisen (or not) in relation to an organism we merely call "a man" or "a woman", "boy" or "girl"? My answer would be that it is not—and that our differing judgements arise on the basis of what we know of ourselves. We *might* be wrong about inferring "purposiveness" in the case of everybody else. But we could not be wrong in the case of ourselves. Sometimes we arrange the stones purposefully. At other times, we might do it under social pressures, hypnotic influences, or by biochemical stimulation.

4. *Could a machine display "consciousness"?*

Mr Dorling rightly lists four clear, important, and necessary conditions for saying, "I am conscious of my heartbeats", or at least for using such a phrase as "being conscious of heart beats". I further agree that in the case of other people it may be logically impossible ever to formulate what is extra when *we* talk of *their* being "conscious". But when *I* talk of *myself* being "conscious" of *x*, *y*, *z*, does it not mean much more, and any claim for the extra in the case of other people arises basically from our own case. It is true that to say that someone is "unconscious" is certainly to say that they are not in an important way reacting to stimuli. But it is *also* to say that they are not, in an important way, like myself.

Further, the question, "Have you any reason to suppose that consciousness is possessed by other people than yourself?", is *not* unanswerable unless we look for knock-down answers. But the start of any answer must certainly be with ourselves.

5. Can the Christian ever suppose that there could be machines which might show emotions—rage, fear, excitement, desire?

I should say: Of course he can. Machines might *show* all that these words mean in terms of observable behaviour. But whether we could say that the machines "had" the emotions as we might say "*I* had" the emotions, is the point at issue. Could a machine display genuine, i.e. self-disclosed, ownership?

Further, let me say that in all this I would never use, as an argument against the possibility of certain developments in cybernetics, the argument that the question was very complex and that a machine of such complexity had not yet been produced, and so on. This sort of argument is no better than the rock pigeon argument we mentioned in question 1. I agree with Mr Dorling that we must in no way laugh the matter away as too fantastic for words.

6. Could a machine of some highly developed form preach a sermon?

This seems to me to be an excellent question and to pin-point the issues. I would like to make three points by way of an answer.

a. Plainly a machine could utter sermonizing words. But,

as everyone would agree, that would not normally be called preaching a sermon.

b. What then is "preaching a sermon"? Some might say: It is to mediate God by the use of words. Certainly the machine could do this. It would then preach a sermon as the external world might preach a sermon—the lilies of the field, the valleys standing full of corn, or the floods and great deeps.

c. But why should a sermon be preached if no "person" could hear? What would be the point of sermons preached by machines to machines? Such exercises might well stir machines to drop out more money, to need less oil, to be stacked more compactly. But all these are contemporary features which may result from sermons, and these we vigorously reject as being the *only* point of sermons. We condemn sermons that are *merely* money-raisers, *mere* stimulants to morale, *mere* dispensers of *esprit de corps*.

We may well recognize a leading question as arising from this whole discussion. It is: Can a scientific account exhaustively treat of persons—in particular of ourselves? This is certainly the central question we must face up to and we cannot brush it away.

As I have said already[1]—and it seems to me to be for the religious man an absolutely necessary answer—I would claim that such a scientific reduction of personality is not possible, and this on logical grounds. All language and all experience presuppose a subject–object distinction which an affirmative answer would deny.

But people then ask, and understandably: What, however, is left? Suppose some area is progressively better and better covered by scientific developments. Must not such developments eventually cover the whole area, and then be completely adequate? But this is not the only picture we may have of scientific developments, and my point would be that it is a badly misleading picture. What then do I propose to substitute for it? What we must picture, in some alternative fashion, is rather ourselves as what each of us realizes himself to be in certain

[1] See pp. 39f, above.

cases of decisive activity, cases which the existentialists often quote—though I would not wish to be restricted only to their colourful examples. My suggestion is that we must picture ourselves as (say) a three-dimensional figure, which has the possibility of an infinite number of two-dimensional projections, representing what any and all scientific accounts of us talk about. This is only a picture, but it is more adequate, I suggest, than the other, in so far as it preserves an irreducible measure of self-transcendence with the possibility of unending scientific elucidation.

I am often accused of wanting both too much and too little. Too much, because I want more than science can talk about, even when there is no end to the story (or stories) science can tell. Too little, because my opponents want a counterpart world containing particular objects labelled "souls". But this latter view seems to safeguard Christian convictions by having a theology which is both irrelevant and unintelligible. I hope I have said enough to establish a *via media*.

Mr Dorling rightly acknowledged at the start that all this challenging work in physiology and psychology was based on two presuppositions,[1] which I venture to reformulate.

The one presupposition amounts to saying that we could give a completely adequate scientific account of human behaviour and human experience. My reply to this is that it supposes third person, impersonal, object language to be adequate about everybody *including myself*. It does not do justice to our own subjectivity. Is not the presupposition of all language and experience that there is an irreducible "I"?

The other presupposition would restrict us to only one "explanation". I see no reason for this. I put no limit on scientific explanation, nor do I suggest that we begin to use religious language where psychology leaves off. But what I am suggesting is that we must use *both* religious language *and* the language of physiology and psychology if we are to give an adequate account of human behaviour. Certainly the more we develop the latter brand of language, the more novelty does it provide for religious people to be exercised about.

[1] See p. 50, above. I have rather inverted the order.

So let me end with a picture conjured up in and around this discussion. How would such a world as Mr Dorling has portrayed to us as a logical possibility, differ from our present world, or would it not differ at all? Suppose scientific developments had occurred of the far-reaching kind we have envisaged. More, suppose we had in fact a universe of nothing but machines, machine-producing machines, weeping machines, laughing machines, and so on. Where would that world differ from this? My answer would be that it would have nothing of characteristically personal experience, no subjectivity; it would display no words which are now currency for "personal backing", and the language we now use of characteristically personal experiences would become superfluous. Nothing would "break in" on a machine as it practised Cartesian methodological doubt;[1] no machine could exercise "decisive" moral activity in some complex issue; a machine could never love another machine for "himself" or "herself". Indeed, all *our* talking *about* such a world—like the very distinction between "men" and "machines"—presupposes a brand of discourse which could not arise in what was no more than a machine-world. There may some day be such a world, but it could not (logical "could not") talk about itself by means of the language which we possess here and now.

We might even summarize and conclude our reflections by saying that the religious man may base his claim that he is more than a machine on the characteristic features which this language of ours here and now displays. The cyberneticists (I agree) do not necessarily explain away, but they are certainly guilty of explaining rather too well.

[1] Some readers may recall the *Punch* cartoon of the perplexed cyberneticists who take from the machine a puzzling tape: "Cogito, ergo sum." To laugh with the cartoon is to see the point about a machine's limitations which I am making above.

3

Dare a Religious Man be a Scientist?

In the first two chapters I was arguing for a kinship between religion and science. In Chapter 1 I suggested that science, as a search for invariants, is rooted in disclosures and appeals to intuition. If then we wish to mediate between those who would say that such invariants are merely jingles, typographical conveniences—whereupon the characteristic categories of science seem to be talking about nothing at all—and those who would say on the other hand that all invariants describe and label something—thus cluttering the world up with all sorts of incompatible furniture—if we wish to have an alternative to both these positions we have somehow to find a currency for what these disclosures associated with invariants distinctively reveal. I then gave reasons for thinking of this distinctive reference in personal terms, so that science becomes suggestive of a personal dialogue with the universe. Such a view seems obviously congruous with belief in God. But that appearance would prove to be only an illusion if in fact "person" were not a religious category at all. If personality were no more than a scientific term, however complex, the use of this concept would not take us a single inch nearer to belief in God.

So in Chapter 2 we faced a crucial question, "What is Man?" Is personality something of which science can exhaustively treat? Large-scale physics, psychosomatic medicine, cybernetics, all these developments seemed on the face of it to leave no place for religion in their implications for human personality. And yet, on the other side, the very vastness of the universe could evoke a mysterious disclosure, a worship in which man, whether the psalmist or Sir Arthur Eddington, has often found his religious significance. Further, even the psychiatrist allowed for a complementary use of specifically religious ministrations in some specific cases. Thirdly, however far-reaching and however valuable developments in cybernetics might be in furthering brain research and the study of human behaviour—and let me emphasize in parenthesis that I deny neither the importance nor the value of the contributions cybernetics has to make in either field—no one would ever produce a machine, which, to put it picturesquely, is indistinguishable from himself. Less picturesquely, no mathematical treatment of the kind which unites the calculating machine and the human brain, no matter how far it goes—and it can go very far indeed—will exhaustively describe human thinking, still less human behaviour, for then we should have objectified the subject. In any case, to take no more than a scientific view of man was, we saw, to raise insuperable problems in relation to man's freedom and responsibility. Cheered, then, by these counter-arguments, and further cheered by various problems, all of which suggested that no scientific account of man could ever be adequate, we argued more positively that man—what we subjectively find ourselves to be when a disclosure occurs such as that which occurred when David came to himself before Nathan—man, known in such a disclosure, is his scientific observable behaviour *and more*. Such a man is indeed "religious". For that is what we mean by calling anything "religious" in the fundamental, basic sense of that word. Whatever transcends the spatio-temporal is a "religious" topic.

In those ways, in the last two chapters, I have argued for a basic kinship between science and religion; and even for the benefits that might accrue to civilization from a recognition of that kinship. But have we overlooked certain important differences between science and religion? What of those who say there are features of scientific method to which I have hardly referred, which make the scientist necessarily irreligious? Dare a religious man be a scientist? That is our question in this chapter.

Now what is this great alleged stumbling-block, which,

some would say, necessarily prevents a religious man from becoming a scientist? What is this feature of scientific method that some would say is dangerous for the religious man to have anything to do with? The answer is: experimental verification, and it is with this that our discussion will be concerned in the first part of the present chapter.

First, let us ask: what *is* the experimental method? What is "experimental verification" as the scientist knows it? Let me illustrate it by three simple examples.

a. Suppose we have discovered, in ways we discussed in Chapter 1, the invariant, 100° Centigrade, for boiling water. Then we can *deduce* that this water here and now in this lab. at this particular time boils at 100° Centigrade. This is something which can be *verified* precisely. Already we have the three stages characteristic of scientific procedure: the generalization expressing some invariant; the deduction; the verification.

b. The second example is a little more complex. Suppose we assume that an invariant between all magnetic substances consists in minute molecular magnets so that a rectangular piece of such a substance could be pictured as follows:

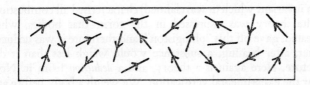

There is obviously no *harm* in picturing a magnetic substance like that; harm would only arise if we were to suppose that these molecular magnets existed "in fact". But that is no part of our case. We are only symbolizing the invariant in all magnetic substances as minute magnets such as the diagram details. From this "hypothesis" we may then *deduce* that when all the minute magnets are mixed up quite indiscriminately as in the diagram there is no magnetism: and this in fact we *verify* when we find a magnetic substance devoid of magnetism. But if we found a way of stroking such a piece of magnetic substance so that all the molecular magnets could be encouraged to point in the same direction, we might expect to finish with a magnet displaying the appropriate north and south poles; the end-product being represented as follows:

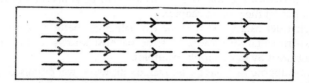

This is again a *deduction* from the hypothesis. If, now, we later disturbed the minute magnets, e.g. by hammering or heating, the magnetism ought to disappear. Here is another *deduction* from the theory. We now set out to test our deductions: we do some stroking, followed by some knocking, alternatively by some heating. All our deductions are verified. The magnetism appears (as we expected) when the magnetic substance is stroked and it disappears (as we expected) when it is heated or knocked about. We have *verified* our hypothesis experimentally.

c. There was a time when the word "phlogiston" referred to an invariant which (it was claimed) characterised all combustion. The theory was expressed in the form that bodies, when heated, gave off this "phlogiston", and therefore it was deduced that, after heating, a substance would weigh less than it did before. Here again is a theory, and a *deduction* from it. Now for the experimental verification. We weigh a body before and after heating, and we discover that our expectation was wrong. The body, after heating, does *not* weigh less than it did before. Therefore we conclude that our original supposition was wrong. Here was a supposition; a deduction from it was *not verified*; and therefore (it is concluded) the original supposition was wrong.

Now it is true that there were some who, to overcome this difficulty, attributed to phlogiston a negative weight. If then, on heating, a body loses phlogiston, it loses negative weight, which means that it will gain in weight; this new deduction is then verified, and the theory seems to be sound after all. But from the point of view of experimental science, this was thought on the whole to be a most unsatisfactory move.[1] Ingenious tinkering with the generalizations to make the deductions fit the facts and for no other reason, is scientifically suspect. It is an important point to bear in mind when presently we have a look at theology.

Here then is experimental verification as it occurs in scientific method. From a theory or a generalization, sharp, precise deductions must be able to be made in detail and subsequently verified. If they are not verified the theory or generalization falls, or (more accurately) is greatly weakened. Here is scientific reasoning: crisp, clear, precise, and appealing in the end to observable fact. Why have religious people been scandalized over this experimental method?

Three reasons have been given, and the third is fortunately better than the first two.

a. The first objection claims that scientific method, and the experimental method in particular, panders to man's selfish desire for human mastery. The scientist (it is said) wants to know everything, and is so blatantly pleased with himself when he finds it out. To quote Francis Bacon, man seeks, in science, to be "lord and oppressor of nature". Now I confess that I find it fearfully difficult to see any point at all in this first attack, and I only give it because apparently intelligent and clear-minded men have often put it forward. I find it very difficult to see anything in the argument which makes it specially relevant to the experimental method of science. I cannot see how anyone is more selfish in wanting to know precisely how far all water boils at 100° Centigrade and then using this knowledge, than in wishing to know precisely all the genitive plurals of all the Latin nouns of the third declension and then putting this knowledge to a good use. I think an equally selfish eye might

[1] Whether or not the concept of negative weight might have led to novel developments in the mathematics of chemical reactions had scientists persisted with the phlogiston theory (as Dr Mascall once remarked to me in conversation) is a most interesting and far-reaching suggestion. But it was of course not a possibility foreseen at the time nor is this the place to consider it further now.

well light up when the classicist discovers on some odd stone in some old backyard in Rome a genitive ending (say) in -aum instead of either -um or -ium. In any case, the scientist surely submits to the facts as readily, or as equally unreadily, as his classical colleague. Pride is no peculiarly scientific vice. So I see nothing in this first argument at all, the argument that verification by experiment encourages man's selfish desires for human mastery.

b. Without further ado, let us pass to what is said to be the second difficulty. The experimental method, we are told, is irreligious because man puts nature to the test. He compels nature to answer his questions, man's questions. Once again, Francis Bacon comes into the argument. Did not Bacon speak of knowledge as power, with the aim of the New Academy the "putting of nature to the question", and such a one as my friend, the late Mr M. B. Foster, comments that this, "in the language of the seventeenth century, meant extracting information by the methods of the Inquisition".[1] Putting nature to the test, putting nature to the question—this, it is said, is what the experimental method involves. The scientist subjects nature to the worst features of the Inquisition.

But science has travelled a very long way since Francis Bacon. The scientist puts his questions to nature all right, but what he tests is not nature, but his own insight, and this can be a very humiliating experience—not for nature, but for the scientist! I cannot see how we can possibly compare scientific inquiry with the Inquisition when we recall how ready the scientist is to change his mind, to reform his views, to replace one invariant by another. In any case, as we have seen in earlier chapters, scientific procedure to-day can be very easily pictured as a conversation with, a dialogue with, the universe, whereas, from all one gathers of the Inquisition, there was very little edifying dialogue about it. So far, then, I think it is rather difficult to take this charge seriously—this charge that the scientist, in his use of experimental method, is being irreligious, displaying spiritual pride, submitting nature to an Inquisition.

[1] *Mystery and Philosophy* (1957), p. 58.

c. But now arises a very important difference and divergence between science and theology. *Scientific method, in formulating verifiable deductions, has a procedure to which there is no theological parallel and which is quite unlike the theologian's attitude to nature.* There are nothing like verifiable deductions in theological method. Let me take three examples to illustrate the difference.

If we drive around the countryside in spring we will probably see little signs popping over the hedges with captions such as this: "This field has been sprayed with Bloggin fertilizer. Watch for a bumper crop." Now here is an invitation to do a verifiable deduction. Supply the suppressed premise: "Bloggin fertilizer produces unparalleled growth" and the conclusion is deduced: "The crop will be a bumper crop." Next time we pass in the car we can look and verify it, or otherwise. So far so good. But we never see notices: "This field is being prayed for regularly by St Mark's. They have an unparalleled number of Easter communicants. Watch for a bumper crop." Something apt and useful for scientific advertising seems a pointless blunder—if not sheer blasphemy—in theology.

Again, suppose it is agreed that God can be described as infinitely loving. Never let us mind for the moment how complex the logic of that assertion may be. Suppose for the sake of the present argument that it is straightforward. "God is infinitely loving." Deduce, therefore: "He won't let my child suffer." But the child, a promising, happy child, does in fact die of some rare disease after prolonged suffering. The conclusion would seem to be that, as in the phlogiston case, the supposition was mistaken. In the one case phlogiston is not given off in combustion. In the other case, God is not infinitely loving. Now it is only fair to say that some people would in fact assert that conclusion. But, however sympathetic we might wish to be to people in such distress as this, we could not admit in a cool hour that "God is not infinitely loving" is a legitimate theological conclusion. In sympathetic understanding the theologian will say, to avoid that conclusion, that we need to clarify in various ways what we mean by "God is infinitely loving". But the important point is that, from a scientific standpoint, any such move to amend the initial premise must be, as in the phlogiston case, exceedingly suspect. What is *de rigueur* in theological reasoning is suspect in science. Suspect and rejected in science, legitimate and practised in theology.

So to the third illustration of apparent tension between science and theology. You may say: "Do not let us be so sophisticated. The religion of Moses and Elijah is good enough for me." But what happened with Elijah in his controversy with the prophets of Baal?[1] Here, you may say, with Professor John Wisdom,[2] was an experimental issue in theology if anything ever was. "Elijah came near unto all the people, and said, How long halt ye between two opinions? If the Lord be God, follow him; if Baal, then follow him. And the people answered him not a word. Then said Elijah unto the people, I, even I only, am left a prophet of the Lord, but Baal's prophets are four hundred and fifty men. Let them therefore give us two bullocks; and let them choose one bullock for themselves, and cut it in pieces, and lay it on the wood, and put no fire under: and I will dress the other bullock, and lay it on the wood, and put no fire under. And call ye on the name of your god, and I will call on the name of the Lord: and the God that answereth by fire, let him be God.[3] . . . And it came to pass at the time of the offering of the evening oblation, that Elijah the prophet came near and said, O Lord, the God of Abraham, of Isaac, and of Israel, let it be known this day that thou art God of Israel. Hear me, O Lord, hear me. . . . Then the fire of the Lord fell, and consumed the burnt offering, and the wood, and the stones, and the dust, and licked up the water that was in the trench."[4] Do we have here a verifiable deduction? It looks on the face of it as though we have, and (as we have noticed) John Wisdom has certainly called it an experimental issue. But was it? Let us notice three points. First, no generalization is ever formulated.

---

[1] I Kings 18.21–39.
[2] "Gods", in A. G. N. Flew, ed., *Logic and Language*, Vol. I (1951), p. 187.
[3] I Kings 18.21–4.
[4] I Kings 18.36–9.

Could Elijah indeed have *deduced* with logical necessity from any specific Jewish doctrines of God that God would send fire that particular day around those particular trenches of water? Hardly. Therefore I am bound to say that there does not seem to me here any question of verifying a deduction. The second point, however, is that, paradoxically enough, Elijah seems, as a religious man, to be doing the very thing about which protests were made earlier, viz., putting God to the test, in the way that no scientist, I should have thought, would ever do. In other words, *if* this were an experimental issue, it would be the most irreligious brand we could ever devise. That is why the religious man will say that it is not an experimental issue, but that Elijah is only seeking God's answer in prayer. Elijah is not verifying deductions, he is yielding himself in prayer, and trusting God for some—no matter what—visible answer.

As the third point, let us ask a question about Elijah which is not often asked: Was it better that God, so to say, "obliged"? I am bound to say, quite honestly, and I hope I may say it without irreverence, that I doubt whether it was. Suppose God *always* obliged as he did that afternoon, what would be the result? God would become no more than (at best) a super-scientific invariant, from which any and every deduction could be certain to be verified. To put the point otherwise: when God obliged that day, he surely laid on Elijah a much greater necessity than ever before for Elijah to be theologically circumspect. In many ways Elijah, we might say, might have had his religion in the long run enriched, if God had not displayed himself so vigorously and so verifiably on that afternoon. We may indeed recall that it was in failing to find anything resembling, let alone anything able to be misunderstood as resembling, verifiable deductions that Jeremiah's religion rose to new and distinctive heights.

Here then, without doubt, is a feature of scientific method which at first sight seems hard to reconcile with such logical moves as are appropriate to a religious attitude. But let us look somewhat further into it. Can we, or can we not, derive verifiable deductions from theological assertions? Let us look more closely at science and theology and their logical relations.

71

In science, you recall, a verifiable deduction is only made because and when an invariant grounded in observations is generalized in some assertion given in a moment of insight. Such an invariant arises (we saw in Chapter I) when a disclosure grows out of a certain pattern of observations, e.g. water boiling, which can then be extrapolated (in the deduction) to continue the pattern.[1]

The following diagram may perhaps summarize the suggestion I am making:

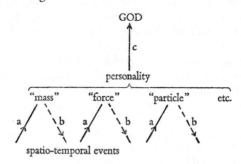

a: words as arising in relation to a disclosure;
and b: words as giving rise to verifiable deductions;
c: personality as the integrating category which may provide some sort of logical clue to the behaviour of the word "God".

Now in this way a scientific invariant is, so to say, betwixt and between. Its relation with spatio-temporal events and observations, so to say "downwards", is straightforward and plain. But its relation, so to say "upwards", to a disclosure, is always and inevitably problematical. It must be, we saw, from this standpoint, more than a jingle, yet it must not describe anything. Our best suggestion was that it is suggestive of, and witnesses upwards to, hints at a personal interchange. We may say indeed that it is when we take all and every invariant and their attached pattern of events, that they

[1] Incidentally, the old problem of induction is thus seen to be the problem of translating insight into a reliable generalization.

72

can witness to God, to talk of whom there is then the suggestion that we use language modelled on the logical behaviour of "I". "God" on this view—and it arises naturally from the picture I have been building up in earlier chapters—thus names that invariant which is anchored objectively in a disclosure situation, when that situation involves the whole universe. At that stage, when nothing is excluded from our vision, we aptly use of God the term "Creator", and *ex nihilo* denotes that there is nothing that the disclosure does not include.

So we have all kinds of scientific events which give rise, in disclosures, to all kinds of invariants. "Downwards" these invariants are cashed readily into verifiable terms, observations similar to those from which they arose; "upwards" they are (as we have seen) suggestive of personality. Further, when the whole universe is gathered together in a disclosure from which nothing is excluded, in relation to *that* disclosure the phrase "Creator God" is commended, and the word "God" has a logical behaviour that can be modelled, usefully as I have said, on the word "I", without of course necessarily claiming logical identity.[1]

Now in what more precise way does the logical behaviour of the word "God" resemble that of "I"? Well, let us look first at this word "I". The word "I" is given in a disclosure situation, which, when it occurs, assures us, as we saw in Chapter 2, of our characteristic subjectivity.[2] It is a disclosure situation which subjectively justifies the use of phrases such as "I exist", "I am alive", "I'm I". But let us notice, *because this is absolutely crucial*, that from such assertions as "I'm I", "I exist", "I am alive", from those assertions, we can make *no* precisely verifiable deductions. Whatever fact you describe about me now, might have been otherwise. There is no logical necessity for any verifiable fact to belong to me now. My hair is white. It might have been—with

[1] Perhaps I ought to emphasize that I am not concerned in this book to discuss the full plotting of the word "God"; if I were, important qualifications would need making to establish its idiosyncratic character and uniqueness. The point is touched somewhat on p. 85.

[2] See p. 42, above.

deference to the ladies—blue with powder. My suit is grey—it might have been pink. My pulse is 60—its value could have been quite different. I have got inhibitions, x, y, z; they might have been alpha, beta, gamma. No detailed assertion that can be made about me can be *deduced rigorously* from the fact that I exist. On the other side, however, all sorts of scientific assertions entail "I exist", i.e. there is entailment in the opposite direction. When the mathematician says of me, "He is executing circular motions with such and such angular velocity and with a centrifugal force on his partner which raises her feet 45° to the vertical"—his assertion will entail (if I am on the dance floor) "I exist". When the physiologist says, "He has a blood count of such and such", it entails (if I am in the clinic) "I exist". When the psychiatrist says, "He is a psychopath", it entails (if I am on the couch) "I exist". When the educationalist says, "He has an I.Q. of 55", it entails (if I am in the form-room) "I exist". All these scientific assertions entail, as a matter of logical necessity, that I exist. But "I exist" *entails* none of these verifiable deductions. We may represent the position like this: "I exist" $\rightleftharpoons$ "He has a temperature of 97.9°." Now, on our general background,[1] the case of God is similar. From "God exists" nothing verifiable can be logically deduced. This is a linguistic way of putting the old theological point that the world is not necessary to God. Yet (we would say) from the world and all the diverse areas of scientific events, God's existence is entailed, and this again is a linguistic way of putting the old theological point that, while the world is not necessary to God, God is necessary to the world. But nothing verifiable in detail can be *deduced* from an assertion of God's existence, any more than it can be *deduced* from an assertion about my existence. The theological case, as I have said, is illuminated by a personal parallel. We may express the logical point by saying that "God exists" is a presupposition of all verifiable, scientific assertions and represent the position somewhat as before: "God exists" $\rightleftharpoons$ "Such and such circumstances are the case."

[1] See pp. 69–71, above; also I. T. Ramsey, "Religion and Science: a philosopher's approach", in *Church Quarterly Review*, Jan. 1961.

Now what do we conclude from these reflections, to which our discussion of the experimental method in science has led us? Two points:

a. We now begin to recognize that despite, and not at all denying, the kinship we stressed between religion and science, there is a vast logical difference between the behaviour of theological and scientific words. From theological assertions no verifiable deductions can be made; from scientific ones they can and must be.

b. And yet in the same breath we must assert that these two diverse logical areas—the theological and the scientific—can be united together on the basis of logical clues supplied by the behaviour of the word "I".

At this point we may recall those two views on the inter-relation of science and religion which I held over from Chapter I.[1]

a. The first view, you remember, argued that scientific language could expand more and more to cover and absorb all that religious language talks about. The bow, seen by Noah, could be adequately dealt with in terms of the composite character of white light and refraction. A Bath-Qol—"voice from heaven"—considered to be thunder, is no more than the inrush of air following the electrical discharge that we call lightning. But these reductions proposed by the physicist are not at all convincing, for (as we now see) they are impersonal substitutes for religious language which is distinctively personal. On the contrary, because and in so far as the logic of religious language is distinctively personal, not only is it never absorbed by scientific language, it can even interlock with and unite any and all scientific language that we devise. The word "God", something like the word "I", interlocks with any and every scientific assertion that can be made about a particular situation. But, you may say, how does religious language contrive to be distinctively personal? Well, let us take some examples and reflect on the words that are definitive of the whole narrative.

---

[1] See p. 5, above.

Consider e.g. Genesis 9.13, "I do set my bow in the cloud", at which point the physicist begins to talk, and rightly, about the composite character of white light, and about reflection and refraction. But the story continues: "It shall be for a token of a covenant between me and the earth." A covenant—here is a characteristically personal word. Or consider John 12.28: "There came a voice out of heaven, saying, I have both glorified it (sc. my name) and will glorify it again." Notice: a voice, conversation. In this way religious language again centres on the *personal* features that this situation possesses. But we now read in a subsequent verse: "The multitude therefore that stood by and heard it said it had thundered." It is interesting that here in the Fourth Gospel, embedded in the very text, are two different accounts which are nevertheless each, in its own right, allowed. The personal and the scientific are locked together in the same situation, and there is no question of the scientific account being denied by the religious story, still less of its being likely to absorb it.

So we conclude this first reflection by denying that the language of science could ever expand so as to deal with all that religious language talks about. For religious language is grounded in the personal, and we have now seen that the personal is not only a category which is never wholly reducible to scientific terms, but that (more positively) it interlocks with all the diverse languages of science to unite them as a common presupposition.

b. To take up the second reflection we held over, and granting the logical diversity between theology and science which we have readily admitted, there is no need whatever, as did the second reflection, to represent the diversity as an utter dichotomy. Indeed (as we have already anticipated) we can go further. Not only must we refuse to make the logical diversity ultimate. More positively, it is precisely because the word "God" has its own peculiar logical behaviour, a behaviour only approached by the word "I", that the languages of science can be significantly united by assertions incorporating the word "God", whereupon the old vision and hopes of science for one large-scale map of the universe again are justified, despite the increasing fragmentation of science. Science, as we have seen, deals in a whole host of models; it embraces invariants of the greatest logical diversity. But in so far as assertions incorporating the word "God", like those incorporating "I", can interlock with any and all scientific assertions, these invariants, these models, these techniques of science, can be reasonably and significantly associated and reconciled by theology. Theology may once again become if not a "Queen" at least a "President" of the sciences.

Let me explain something of what lies behind these last remarks, as well as what justifies them, by making a rather long but not, I hope, an irrelevant, digression. What I propose to do in effect, in a sort of parenthesis, is to give a somewhat popular introduction to what Bertrand Russell called the Theory of Types, what has sometimes and since been talked of in terms of category differences. Let me begin with a few illustrations. Suppose we are sitting round a fire one winter's evening with an old friend, warm and relaxed, and talking over our favourite authors by the firelight: "I do love the Bishop of Barchester." ... "So do I." ... "By Jove, wasn't his wife, Mrs Proudie, a tartar?" ... "Not half." ... Silence. ... Then a few minutes afterwards—"Fancy treating the Archdeacon like that." ... "Oh I can believe anything—she once stayed with us!" Our friend is dumbfounded—"Waken up, old chap, you're confounding the languages of fiction and sense experience. What you've just uttered—'She, i.e. Mrs Proudie, once stayed with us'—is technically nonsense. It unites two logically diverse areas, the language of fiction and of sense-experience." Or again, two schoolboys are talking. One says, having recently started the Calculus, "I absolutely love integrals", and the other says, "Do you eat them with vinegar and salt?" Silly? Yes, because it confounds Calculus and shellfish language, and the result is nonsense. Or again, the bright young thing in the British Ministry of Food in the war, who (so the story goes), having seen an advertisement for Bristol Cream and Bristol Milk Sherry, wrote to that well-known firm of sherry importers, Harveys of Bristol, and asked them to let her have promptly by return the percentage of cream and milk they used in the mixture to see if they were contravening some milk and fat regulation. She confounded—dear soul—the language of sherry parties and the language of the Fats division of the Ministry of Food. And the result? A most unedifying correspondence.

Now in this way, we must distinguish, says Russell in effect, areas of language which are logically indigenous and logically compact. We must recognize that discourse is logically variegated; that is one point. Then there is a second point which the examples have already illustrated, but which I will presently exemplify further. A straight mixture of logical areas, when a word from one area trespasses into another and links itself with a native, produces nothing but blundering, which may be stupid, silly, funny, or exasperating, but it is certainly *not* significant. It is, in fact, technically nonsense.

Let me give two more examples of such type-trespass. "I found three wonderful trains at the Great Northern station this afternoon", says the engine-spotter. "Did you now?" we ask. "Yes: a C.I.E. train, a U.T.A. train, and a bridal train." A joke, maybe, but not very edifying. Or again, notice how we can produce the most tangled discourse if we fail to locate categories in their correct logical areas. Someone hears of Robert Boyle, Father of Chemistry and brother of the Earl of Cork, and he says, "Ah, and what was that sweet little fellow like? Dear little Chemistry. He must have been the apple of his uncle's eye, the Earl of Cork. Where is little Chemistry now? Which university did he go to? What did he read?" So the discourse could proceed as what appears a most respectable quest for information, whereas in fact it is utter rubbish. That is what happens when in particular we develop scientific theories at logical cross-purposes—when, for example, we mix models, wave models and particle models, to mention only one example. No wonder the attempt seemed difficult, and did not succeed when scientists tried it. It was a logical blunder even to want to begin.

But do you now see the problem that is emerging for science? If the models, the analogies, the mathematical procedures sponsored by science are as different as they are, science cannot escape logical fragmentation. But then it *cannot* attain to the ideal of one scientific map of the universe by merely linking all the models as if they were homogeneous, for that will lead, as we have seen, to logical rubbish. It will mix categories; it will commit what, following Ryle, we have called "type-trespass."[1] It will confound category differences. How then can science preserve its ideal, seeing that it cannot without absurdity merely mix together its models? It needs assertions which can interlock with scientific assertions and yet not be themselves scientific. It will preserve its ideal only if there are words not native to any of the constituent languages of science, whose logical behaviour is not that of a scientific category, and which yet can interlock with the languages of science to unite them. Where will such words be found? We know the answer already. Precisely in the two we have mentioned: "I" and "God".[2] If the word "God" behaves anything like the word "I", theology, you see, supplies science with the very solution it needed to its problem of fragmentation. *The logical diversity between the languages of religion and science, far from being a hindrance, is a positive merit, indeed it is a logical necessity. For in the long run it enables theology to supply a fragmented science with that one cosmic map which remains the scientific ideal.*

Incidentally, we can now see why, in physics, we shall never find a third theory as an exact substitute for two or more logically diverse theories; why we can be rightly suspect of interpreting too easily what the move to hidden parameters may succeed in doing. It may provide a super-theory to replace the other two, but it *cannot*—and it is a logical "cannot"—provide a scientific link between the original theories, or it will certainly commit type-trespass. On the other hand, as we have seen, the language of religion can grip scientific theories, however diverse, without the least logical embarrassment. The language of religion can indeed be logically polygamous and happy as well.

[1] See e.g. "Categories", by Gilbert Ryle, in *Logic and Language*, ed. A. G. N. Flew, Vol. II (1953), esp. p. 75.
[2] See the logical diagrams on p. 74, which show how "I exist" and "God exists" can provide an integrating centre for scientific assertions.

So while there is an important difference spotlighted by the use in science and not in theology of experimental verification, it is a difference which, *far from* registering a basic incompatibility, is *indeed* in the fullest sense of the word, a "God-send", for it provides for a union of theology and science which does justice to them both and compromises and confounds neither.

We thus have the vision of a compact language map wherein all the diverse languages of science are harmonized, without confounding type differences, and without committing category blunders. It is a map on which assertions incorporating the word "God"—of whose logical behaviour "I" provides some kind of reflection—occupy a central, presiding position, being entailed by, but themselves entailing none of these assertions of natural science; and the whole map is anchored in, and finds its empirical basis in a cosmic disclosure, when we respond to what is disclosed, and what is mediated to us, through the patterns of the natural world. There are indeed some biblical expressions of this "natural religion". If we turn to Genesis 4.16–22, and if we take the genealogies as representing *logical* relations, we can see how we may relate to God the affairs of the city—we might call it economics; to matters of tents and cattle—we might call it scientific agriculture; and to brass and iron—we might call it metallurgy. Or if we go to I Kings 4.29–34,[1] we shall see how "God's wisdom" can be a concept with which there is interlocked Solomon's knowledge about trees, about the cedar that is in Lebanon and about the hyssop that springeth out of the wall: botany; beasts, fowls, creeping things and fishes: biology; and so on. So far, I know, there is nothing specifically Christian about this view, but to indicate where the Christian view would fit, let me just say this. A Christian is he who makes his cosmic commitment and response within a cosmic disclosure which occurs from and around a group of events of which the life, death, and resurrection of Jesus Christ are central. Not that such events stand

[1] Cf. H. St J. Hart, *A Foreword to the Old Testament* (1951), pp. 115–21.

alone, and out of all reference to events of the Old Testament on the one hand and events of the Christian Church on the other; the one, as the Christian consistently says, foreshadows Christ, the other characterizes the "body of Christ". What the Christian does, more than the man who is merely, shall I say "religious", is to set his scientific and natural commitment within a Christian commitment, fulfilling his concept of God as Creator with a concept of God as Redeemer. And if we look for the Christian counterpart of the "natural religion" of, say, Genesis 4 and 1 Kings 4, we may perhaps find it in such passages as Ephesians 1.10, where God's purpose is described as "to sum up all things" (including "the things upon the earth") "in Christ", or in Colossians 1.16,17, "In him [i.e. in Christ] were all things created."

Before passing to my concluding remarks, it may I think help if I now outline in broad perspective the overall view which I have set out, rather intricately I fear, in the last few pages.[1] It is a view which, far from minimizing the logical differences between theology and science, sees in these very differences the possibility of a unified map. But this approach to synthesis through conflict may seem rather bewildering. So let me endeavour a brief overall recapitulation which incidentally may link together more firmly the first chapter and this one.

In Chapter 1 I suggested that the scientist, in pursuing his trade, needs for his theories invariants such as "particle" or "mass" which are neither descriptive labels nor mere jingles, but which in one way or another arise originally from, and so witness to, insight or a disclosure in virtue of which, if he so wishes, the scientist may regard his activity as leading to God. As a scientist, however, he need not face these wider philosophical issues; he need not take his invariants as anything more than jingles. But if he is ever tempted to spread himself and to cultivate his invariants he will certainly be wise not to take them as descriptions. He will recall, for example, that many of the questions clustering around the old problem of the wave versus particle theories of light arose quite unnecessarily

[1] Pp. 73–81.

because they were expressed in terms of the question as to how any one thing could be both a wave and a particle at the same time. To this extent the traditional problem was quite bogus, resting as it did on the supposition that wave mechanics, and particle mechanics described things. There was of course a genuine problem involved, viz. how to unite wave mechanics and particle mechanics into one comprehensive system. But it was only a pseudo-problem that puzzled itself as to how to combine the diverse facts which these different languages were supposed to *describe*. At the end of Chapter 1 the alternative suggestion was made that the ultimate reference for scientific invariants, grounded in disclosures, might have something of a personal character—where "personal", as we came to see in Chapter 2, had religious, because transcendent, overtones.

Now in the present chapter I have emphasized that not only may a scientist legitimately neglect for his immediate professional purposes the disclosure basis of his central concepts, he most characteristically indulges in deductive verification of a kind which theology, interested primarily in the disclosures, cannot sponsor. At this point it might seem that the two attitudes were quite other and diverse. But as I have also emphasized in this chapter, the assertion "God exists" has a logic similar in important respects to that of the phrase "I exist", being grounded in a disclosure, though this time of a cosmic kind. No one can therefore expect that language about God, any more than the first-person assertions it resembles, will generate deductions capable of empirical verification. It happens, however, that this very peculiarity attaching to the logical character of "God exists" enables it, without generating the nonsense of category-confusion, to be linked with, as a presupposition of, all empirical assertions. Further, providing in this way a supplement for scientific languages, theology then does justice to that disclosure basis of science which scientists for the most part legitimately overlook and neglect. Incidentally, on this full perspective it is then not surprising that science in its more general exposition makes use of personal phrases, as we saw in Chapter 1. We begin indeed to see something of the full logical significance of those phrases, and that they are not rightly understood if they are supposed to be no more than vague flights of a weak analogy.

Here then is a synthetic venture which tries to do justice both to the diversity and to the ultimate interlocking of scientific and theological discourse; both to the experimental method in science, and the grounding of scientific invariants in disclosures that are ultimately theological.

Let me now conclude by setting before you just one or two broad considerations which come from the full picture, as I have tried to outline it over these three chapters. First, consider religion. *Religion* sponsors a vision and an affirmation, an affirmation which is an appropriate response to what is disclosed; it sponsors an order in the universe which is at least a personal order. But the *problem* of religion, or more accurately of theology, is, starting from this vision, to get empirical relevance. No verifiable deductions can be made. Not that this is specially distressing—it is merely indicative of what religious loyalty is, and let us recognize in parenthesis that the difficulty recurs, as we might well expect it to recur, in morality. We may recognize duty with a capital D, we may well be aware of an obligation, but very often it is an obligation which defies any exact empirical formulation. Here is what, if we drew up a sort of profit and loss account, might be called the debit side of theology.

Science, on the other hand, has no difficulty over empirical relevance. Its invariants are formulated with an eye to their empirical usefulness and the number of them is legion. Empirical relevance abounds. But the *problem* of science is to fulfil its hope to provide one map of the universe, to find language which will harmonize so many assertions displaying such logical diversity. It seeks after its map by seeking for more and more stable invariants, and as it grasps any one of them, the map to date breaks up into a thousand more fragments. Science seems to have nothing at the end but a whole host of logically isolated areas, and this is the debit side of science.

So it is that the scientist and the religious man, when they come together, receive from each other a benefit, but with the benefit, a liability as well. *Religion gives to science* the vision and the single map for which it searches; but science then pays the price of having in the end categories, theological categories, which elude empirical verification. *Science gives to theology* the broad empirical relevance that it needs. It provides theology with a contemporary culture and moral problems on which it can bring its insight to bear; but theology then pays the price— and pay the price it must—of talking about the world by using language that, like the language of science must be, is tentative, reformable, and without guarantee. Is this shocking? Hardly. The Bible itself is content to set its vision of a Creator God in the context of scientific stories so obviously diverse as those which occur in Genesis 2 and Genesis 1. It was not a scientist and it was not a philosopher, but a very devout biblical scholar, Dr S. R. Driver, who, reflecting on the Creation narratives of Genesis, said, "Upon the false science of antiquity" —I think to-day we would prefer to say inadequate science— "its author has grafted a true and dignified representation of the relation to the world of God."[1] Upon the inadequate sciences of antiquity there was a disclosure of a Creator God. If this troubles and scandalizes us, as to how someone could have a disclosure of a Creator God while seeing through science darkly, let me just say this. Fortunately God never waits until we are perfect in thought and action before he reveals himself to us, and there is, as I see it, basically no more difficulty in believing God to be revealed by an inadequate science, than in believing that, on the human level, the same person can reveal himself to us in vastly different ways—through knowledge less and later more adequate, through hair black and later white, through face youthful and later wrinkled.

Science and religion can be set together: what does it come to in practice? St Mark's fête day arrives and the sun shines warm from a blue sky. Bowling for the pig is poor old Farmer Smith, bent double; the Mothers' Union stall is packed with pots of onions, and sponge cakes in profusion; the ladies of the choir have for sale blouses and jumpers without number; the Youth Club is behind the bushes with its washboard and skiffle group;

[1] *Genesis*, Westminster Commentaries (10th edn, 1916), p. 33.

a great variegation of colour and noise is spread abroad. Swallows fly low across the vicarage lawn. "It's a fine day for the fête", beams the Vicar as he rubs his hands. Says dear and devout Mrs Fildes, "Yes, Vicar, our prayers have been answered." "My comment", says cocky Jim Sparrow, "is that there's an anticyclone over the Channel", for cocky Jim Sparrow has just obtained his O level in G.C.E. geography, and has every hope of reforming the B.B.C. weather forecast when he becomes Director of the Meteorological Office. Are Mrs Fildes and Jim Sparrow in conflict? No. For Mrs Fildes, the variegation of colour, alongside the words of her prayer, has evoked a disclosure. She has found God in the fête. God has spoken to her in the fête as to Noah in the bow, as to our Lord in the thunder: a personal interchange in a restricted context. Indeed, to use the technical term, there has been a "miracle". But Jim Sparrow comes to the fête from the other side. He puts the fête, not alongside his private prayers, but alongside charts of isobars and isotherms, alongside observations of cumulus and cirrus clouds, of humidity and temperature, of electric charges on atmospheric particles, and so on. He does not exclude God: it is merely that he has not yet found God that way, or so we may suppose. But let Jim go on and on, not doing less science but more and more, until, we may trust, in a cosmic disclosure, he finds the Creator God, a God not averse to personal characterization. Jim will then have found something of a divine interchange in a cosmic context; he will have found indeed a God he has known elsewhere in his prayers. Jim Sparrow and Mrs Fildes will then meet together. The fullest account of a miraculous situation embraces both the discernment of particular activity *and* the discernment of a Creator God. As with the writer of Exodus 14 what happened at the Red Sea both led to belief in the Creator God (v. 21: "a strong east wind") and was also discerned as a miracle—a particular activity of God (v. 30: "the Lord saved Israel that day").

So we end. The kinship between religion and science for which I argued in Chapter 1, a kinship which, as I argued in Chapter 2, is significant for contemporary culture—this kinship is in no wise denied by that feature of scientific method, experimental verification, which at first sight seemed so ir-religious. On the contrary, the experimental verification which scientific method characteristically practises not only reminds us of the logical diversity of science and theology, but precisely in doing that it prepares us for the union of all fragmentary scientific languages without involving ourselves in type-tres-pass. For assertions incorporating the word "God", like those incorporating the word "I", or the word "persons", can inter-lock with the assertions of science, and since the word "God" is not native to the language of science this interlocking can occur without logical compromise. Science and religion are thus enabled to meet in what is basically a personal interpreta-tion of the universe, where science finds its hopes fulfilled in theology,[1] and theology is provided with its empirical tasks and relevance by science.

Nor are these themes very new, especially in Ireland. George Berkeley, the great eighteenth-century philosopher-bishop, takes us back to our first chapter when we recall his criticism of Newton's Absolutes, and his shrewd judgement that the logical outcome of Newton's physics was atheism, a judgement which Laplace abundantly confirmed. But Berkeley was positive as well. In his *Alciphron*, he said in effect: we see God as we see persons. Hair, face, skin, all these are visible, but to "see" a *person* is to see these, and more besides.[2] Likewise God. We look on the universe, from galaxies to mesons, from blood sugar to insulin, from points to entropy, from acetic acid to vitamin B, from hydrogen to whatever element at the moment closes the periodic table, and by and through them all, we see God as we see a person, through his hair and face and skin—a person who is all these and more. The world, as Berkeley taught us to look on it, is divine, visual language, and all we need add some two hundred years later is that what the scientist does and

[1] Cf. W. Heisenberg, *Philosophic Problems of Nuclear Science* (1952), p. 26: "Perhaps it is not too rash to hope that new spiritual forces will again bring us nearer to the unity of a scientific concept of the universe which has been so threatened during the last decades."

[2] *Alciphron*, Fourth Dialogue, s. 5 (*Works*, ed. A. A. Luce and T. E. Jessop, Vol. III, p. 147).

what the theologian does, each in his own way, is to discover the logical patterns of this divine visual language as best he can. So I cannot conclude any other way than with a humble tribute to George Berkeley, who was concerned as well for the economic welfare of Ireland as for its cultural and religious life, as well for the universities of the Commonwealth as for philosophy at home, as well for Tar-Water as for the Trinity, as well for medicine as for theology; George Berkeley, sometime Dean of Derry, and later Bishop of Cloyne, a great philosopher, a great Anglican, a great Irishman!

4
Epilogue

Genesis 1.1: God created the heaven and the earth

I DO not think that I have ever seen an account which has been arithmetically convincing of how this Sunday comes to be called Septuagesima. But fortunately all accounts agree on the central point, viz. that the name is forward-looking and some-how linked with Lent and Easter. Whereas during the Epiphany season we have been looking back towards Christmas, to-day we turn to look forward to Lent, Good Friday, Easter Day. From to-day we anticipate Lent—that season when we en-deavour to deepen our faith, to intensify our commitment: and what better preliminary could there be to such renewal than the pondering of God and our creatureliness . . . nature and human nature . . . the cosmic background against which alone God's redemption in Christ can be given its full meaning and significance. Hence it has been traditional, on this Septuagesima Sunday to ponder the God of Nature whose grace and life eternal in Jesus Christ we are to learn anew in Lent; and it is in order to set before us the God of Nature that we have Psalm 104, sing the Benedicite instead of the Te Deum, and have our Old Testament lesson from Genesis 1.

From Nature to Nature's God; to contemplate Nature till we see the Creator . . . this is where those early chapters of Genesis would lead us, and let us see how. For it is a matter in which men have made the most appalling blunders and where the friends of religion have sometimes been more dangerous than its foes, and made men of vision and goodwill atheists and agnostics.

"In the beginning, God created the heaven and the earth." . . . "Created." . . . If we look at the Hebrew original, we notice that the verb is not at all in its customary form. Its root meaning is to cut, or to fashion, and its general use is intensive, implying many cuttings, repeated cuttings, as the workman fashions and shapes a particular model. Normally, in other words, the verb tells of a human maker and constructor, the sculptor or the wood-carver. But in this verse of Genesis, the verb is used in a simple, not an intensive form: it is meant to designate somehow and in some way a power which altogether transcends the power of man, a God whose relation to the world, however much it might be compared to constructing and making, must even more importantly be severely distinguished from those activities. The power of God, of which this unique "creating" speaks, altogether transcends that of the sculptor or the wood-carver, however skilled; of any man, however ingenious.

At the beginning of the Genesis story, then, we have this word "creating". But what *is* "creating"? How are we to understand it? How do we discover that relation between God and the world for which the word stands?

It is the primary purpose of the first chapter of Genesis to provide us with an answer. The word "create" occurs indeed both as a sort of title to the story and also as an epilogue to Genesis 1, and the story between is meant (I suggest) to give the word its meaning. What the narrative does in effect is to give us a technique by which the Creator God may be disclosed. Contemplate the universe, it suggests, in a certain pattern; survey it in certain stages. *Begin* to think of the universe as chaotic as possible—quite ill-defined where no distinctions are visible: without form and void—*tōhū-wā-bōhū*, as the Hebrew labels it —something like our "higgledy-piggledy". Then the first signs of order and classification emerge—light and darkness associated with the phrase "Let there be light!" Notice in particular the logical importance of the imperative. We all know how an imperative can produce order: the children in the playground running and shouting, an absolute chaos of movement and noise—and then: the Master's whistle; or as he comes into a dishevelled form-room: "Silence!" "Let there be silence!" . . . and the schoolyard or room possesses an order it lacked before. Contemplate then the transition from chaos to order, however primitive . . . associate this (says the writer in effect) with an imperative, where the imperative recalls declarations of a personal will. As the school imperatives make us aware of a master, as they disclose his presence . . . do we not catch a glimpse of the "Creator" likewise? As the pattern is developed and new order emerges, an imperative is regularly brought alongside, and at each stage the author hopes that such a disclosure may occur as reveals the Creator God, as discovers to us that on which the whole universe depends. Night and day; the firmament dividing the waters from the waters; earth distinguished from seas; grass, herbs, and trees; sun and moon; the animals of sky and sea; beasts and cattle and creeping things. Here is a pattern, then, developed with imperatives alongside in the hope that at some stage God the Creator will be disclosed to us. But our account is not yet complete.

For as we come to the end, the story takes a significantly different turn. It does not conclude, as we might have expected, with "Let there be man, and there was man". Rather, "Let us make man". What a difference there is between the phrases "Let there be" and "Let us": from the one emerges an order and pattern whose units are, at least in that context, less than personal—the pattern of the barrack-square or the playground. On the other hand we use the phrase "let us" of activities which are mutually and distinctively personal, where man knows man in fellowship. "Let us go for a walk"; "Let us be friends"; "Let us pray". . . . "Let us make man" is therefore not surprisingly followed by the words "in our own image"—as a personal counterpart such as we see of ourselves in a mirror—someone dependent on *our* being there *indeed*, but moving in perfect harmony with ourselves: "Let us make man in our own image." Let us make man as our dependent counterpart in fellowship with ourselves. Not this time the impersonal language of a third-person imperative; but the first-person imperative which suggests a dialogue, and a response. Not this time a creative fiat

—but creation known in and through a dialogue. Let man discern that which confronts him is his most personal existence: and there he finds the Creator God. *See the story of creation then as giving us, in its succession of days, a pattern which becomes more and more personal, which more and more focuses on to ourselves till our eyes are opened to the God who meets us everywhere and who would that we move in harmony with himself.* Day and night—the physical universe—the earth and skies—our food; sun and moon—the birds—the cattle—ourselves. The aim of the author is to open our eyes at some stage or other to the Creator God with whom we have kinship in and through the physical world. From Nature to Nature's God.

Not that this is an exercise confined, of course, to the Book of Genesis. The writer of Psalm 8 has a similar technique for disclosing the Creator. What is man? What is man as a creature? Well, move *from* man: sheep and oxen and beasts of the field, fowls of the air and fishes of the sea: moon and stars and heavens . . . broaden our perspective till the Creator God is disclosed. Or consider Ps. 104, which surveys light and the heavens; the clouds and the wind, earth and the seas, mountains and valleys; birds and animals, day and night . . . then man. Or recall the Book of Job where in Chapters 38 and 39 the vast panorama of Nature is surveyed—morning star, lightning and thunder, dew and hoar frost, wild goats and ostriches, the horse and the hawk, hippopotamus and crocodile . . . things too wonderful for Job which he knew not. From Nature to Nature's God. "O let the earth bless the Lord: praise him and magnify him for ever."

But a cosmic disclosure may not occur: we may survey the universe and fail to find God. We can even make the mistake of those who are criticized in Wisdom 13. They looked at fire, or wind, or swift air, circles of stars or raging waters; they even took delight in the beauty which these revealed; but their disclosures embraced no more than the finite. They thought these finite objects—impressive, elusive, vast, terrible—to be gods that rule the world. Says the author of Wisdom: "Let them know how much better than these is their sovereign Lord."

How we like to stay with gods of our own making, sometimes concealing only too disastrously the sovereign Lord! That reflection easily takes us back to 1860. It was in that year that there occurred the notorious meeting of the British Association in Oxford when Wilberforce attacked Huxley and the battle seemed to be on between Evolution and Genesis. From what I have said about the Book of Genesis and how it seeks to portray God as Creator, what may we say at this distance of time about that unedifying controversy? In the first place, we cannot too often remind ourselves that even 100 years ago there were notable Churchmen who were not at all dismayed by contemporary scientific developments—such were Archbishop Frederick Temple and Dean Church, to mention only two. But many were dismayed, distressed, and chiefly I believe for two reasons:

First, William Paley, who had taught many generations of Cambridge men and others too to look on Nature like a watch, tempted them to think of God as a most ingenious *artificer and constructor* whose time-sheet or log was Genesis 1. Secondly, Genesis 1 was supposed to be descriptive, and its value stood or fell on the question as to whether its descriptions were true or false. It was as descriptive accounts of the emergence of man that Genesis and Darwinism were in opposition.

Now what are we to say about these two presuppositions?

First I emphasized at the start that the writer of Genesis 1 wished above all else to distinguish God from any ingenious artificer—woodcarver, sculptor, or watchmaker. These at best could be no more than pictures. The religious man can find no satisfaction in the thought of God as starting the do-it-yourself movement, working a twenty-four-hour day and no strikes.

Secondly, we must not suppose that the point of Genesis is to give a descriptive diary of the first days, a sort of *News of the World* coming out on the first Sunday. Plainly it could not be that, if only because no reporters were there to see anything until the sixth day. Its logic, as I tried to outline it earlier, is far more complex. What the author of Genesis does is to use the best scientific language available; to set it in a pattern of imperatives; to arrange that this pattern centres on ourselves, and

93

all this to evoke a disclosure in which God—as Creator—is found. What Wilberforce should have done in the Darwinian controversy was to make a genuine scientific examination of Darwin's views, rather than be led astray by the scientific jealousies of Richard Owen, who was only too anxious to use Wilberforce as a tool. Then Darwinism might have been welcomed in so far as it could bring with it the possibility of new apologetic. In this way, a disclosure story to reveal the meaning of the word "creation" might have been built out of another scientific account of the universe, as Genesis 1 does it with a different story from Genesis 2. For remember: we learn to talk of God *as Creator* when we construct from a scientific story about the universe a technique to evoke a disclosure.

But I cannot close without making one further comment on what seems to me to be the major mistake made by *both* sides in the Darwinian controversy. It is the mistake—indeed the sin —described by Paul in Romans 1.26, to worship the creature rather than the Creator. There was certainly a danger that the Darwinians would remain content with the pattern of natural selection—with nature as their theory organized it—and never use it to evoke a disclosure of God. Further, we have already noted the danger that the religious man might give the language of Genesis no more than a descriptive meaning. Theologians as much as scientists can lack vision. We may be too dogmatic about our science; but it is an even greater sin to deny to religious language its religious significance. That is to worship the creature with a vengeance—to make idols of words.

Was not this the fatal mistake of the Jews? The Law hid rather than revealed God to them. They concentrated on the external criteria of behaviour—and they found themselves in that state called "wrath": a word which for us suggests a state where persons become vested with the impersonal or even the sub-personal. This is the basic mistake—it is also the basic sin. But let him who is without sin cast the first stone. It is as easy to condemn the Wilberforces of a century ago as to overlook our own errors. Let us in our own day not neglect our safeguard. While we endeavour, as best we may in the science of our time, to discover God's presence and power in the stars, the earth, the animals—astronomy, physics, chemistry, botany, physiology, and so on—let us learn that presence and power most distinctively from the disclosure which occurs in Christ, and become thereby not just a creature, but a new creature: with the Creator God revealed anew.

Septuagesima and Genesis, from Nature to Nature's God. Sad to tell, from Nature we may be led no further, and then we are enslaved in the strongest scientific shackles to date; or from Nature we may be led only to a God who is an ingenious artificer, and then we make religious men unbelievers. But we may so read Genesis that it discloses God; and not only encourages us to search for a like consecration of contemporary science, but also prepares us for the fullest disclosure of all in Jesus Christ. In short, we may so read Genesis as to prepare ourselves to learn Christ: when Septuagesima finds its fulfilment in Lent.

Index